ARL ANNUAL SALARY SURVEY 2009–2010

Compiled and Edited by

MARTHA KYRILLIDOU
LES BLAND

ASSOCIATION OF RESEARCH LIBRARIES
WASHINGTON, DC
2010

ARL Annual Salary Survey 2009–2010

The quantitative tables presented in this publication are not indicative of performance and should not be used as measures of library quality. In comparing any individual library to ARL medians or to other ARL members, one must be careful to make such comparisons within the context of differing institutional characteristics.

Custom reports based on the *Salary Survey* data are also available. Contact the ARL Statistics and Measurement Program Officer for further information.

Visit the ARL Statistics and Measurement Program online at http://www.arl.org/stats/.

Published by the
Association of Research Libraries
Washington, DC 20036
www.arl.org

ISSN 0361-5669
ISBN 1-59407-856-4
EAN 978-1-59407-856-9

The paper used in this publication meets the minimum requirements of the American National Standard for Information Science and National Information Standards Organization standard—Permanence of Paper for Publications and Documents in Libraries and Archives, ANSI/NISO Z39.48-1992(R1997).

CONTENTS

US ARL UNIVERSITY LIBRARIES

CANADIAN ARL UNIVERSITY LIBRARIES

ARL UNIVERSITY MEDICAL LIBRARIES

ARL University Law Libraries

Salary Survey Trends 2009–2010

The *ARL Annual Salary Survey 2009–2010* reports salary data for all professional staff working in ARL libraries. The Association of Research Libraries (ARL) represents the interests of libraries that serve major North American research institutions. The Association operates as a forum for the exchange of ideas and as an agent for collective action to influence forces affecting the ability of these libraries to meet the future needs of scholarship. The ARL Statistics and Measurement program, which produces the *Salary Survey*, is organized around collecting, analyzing, and distributing quantifiable information describing the characteristics of research libraries. The *ARL Annual Salary Survey* is the most comprehensive and thorough guide to current salaries in large US and Canadian academic and research libraries, and is a valuable management and research tool.

Data for 10,207 professional staff members were reported this year for the 114 ARL university libraries, including their law and medical libraries (948 staff members reported by 73 medical libraries and 747 staff members reported by 76 law libraries). For the 10 nonuniversity ARL members, data were reported for 3,811 professional staff members.

The tables are organized in seven major sections. The first section includes Tables 1 through 4, which report salary figures for all professionals working in ARL member libraries, including law and medical library data. The second section includes salary information for the 10 nonuniversity research libraries of ARL. The third section, entitled "ARL University Libraries," reports data in Tables 7 through 25 for the "general" library system of the university ARL members, combining US and Canadian data but excluding law and medical data. The fourth section, composed of Tables 26 through 30, reports data on US ARL university library members excluding law and medical data; the fifth section, Tables 31–34, reports data on Canadian ARL university libraries excluding law and medical data. The sixth section (Tables 35–41) and the seventh section (Tables 42–48) report on medical and law libraries, respectively, combining US and Canadian data.

The university population is generally treated in three distinct groups: staff in the "general" library system, staff in the university medical libraries, and staff in the university law libraries. Any branch libraries for which data were received, other than law and medical, are included in the "general" category, whether or not those libraries are administratively independent. Footnotes for many institutions provide information on branch inclusion or exclusion.

In all tables where data from US and Canadian institutions are combined, Canadian salaries are converted into US dollar equivalents at the rate of 1.1667 Canadian dollars per US dollar.[1] Tables 4 and 31 through 34, however, pertain exclusively to staff in Canadian university libraries, so salary data in those tables are expressed in Canadian dollars.

---

[1] This is the average monthly noon exchange rate published in the Bank of Canada Review for the period July 2008–June 2009 and is used in converting figures that are shown effective as of 1 July 2009. This information can be accessed at: http://www.bankofcanada.ca/en/rates/exchange.html.

RACE AND ETHNICITY

There were 1,296 minority professional staff reported in 99 US ARL university libraries, including law and medical.[2] Note that the data for minority professionals comes only from the US ARL university libraries following the Equal Employment Opportunity Commission (EEOC) definitions; Canadian law prohibits the identification of Canadians by ethnic category.

Currently, 14.3% of the professional staff in US ARL university libraries (including law and medical) belongs to one of the four non-Caucasian categories for which ARL keeps records. The percentage of minorities in managerial or leadership positions in the largest US academic libraries is far lower: 6.1% are directors (7 out of 114), 6.3% are associate directors (20 out of 316), 5.3% are assistant directors (9 out of 170) and 9.4% (46 out of 487) are branch librarians (see Table 27). Figure 1, below, depicts the overall racial/ethnic distribution of professional staff in US ARL university libraries: Caucasian/Other 85.7%, Asian/Pacific Islander 6.4%, Black 4.6%, Hispanic 2.8%, and American Indian/Alaskan Native 0.5%.

Figure 1: Ethnicity/Race of Professional Staff in US ARL University Libraries, FY 2009–2010

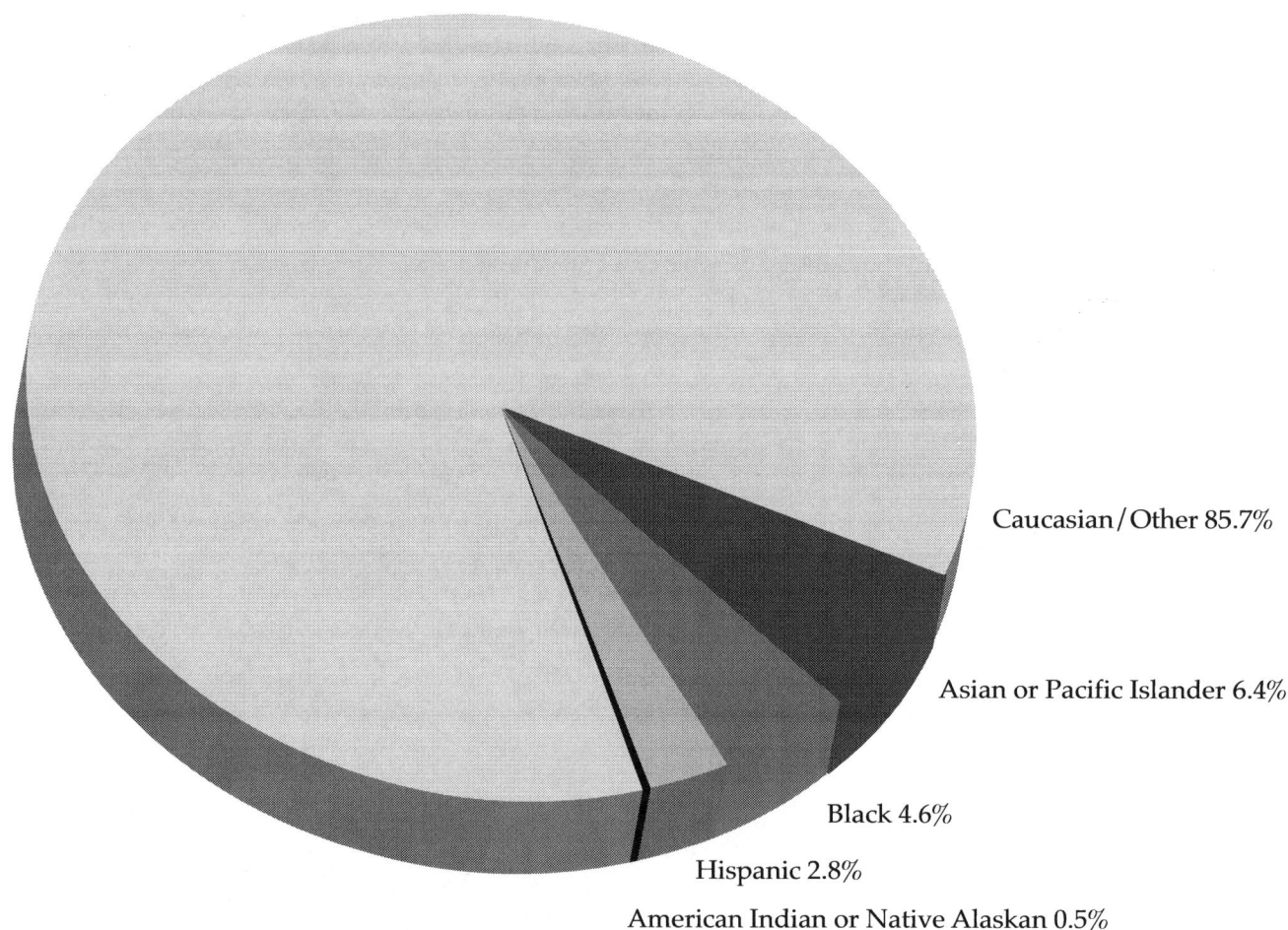

Caucasian/Other 85.7%

Asian or Pacific Islander 6.4%

Black 4.6%

Hispanic 2.8%

American Indian or Native Alaskan 0.5%

---

[2] Some US institutions offer their librarians the option of not reporting race and ethnicity; others forbid the tracking of racial and ethnic classification altogether. See Footnotes.

Minority professional staff in US ARL university libraries continue to be disproportionately distributed across the country. Using Figure 1, we can compare the number of minority staff with other staff, region by region. These patterns of distribution have been relatively stable for the entire history of ARL's data-collection experience. Minorities are most underrepresented in the East South Central, New England, and Mountain regions (see page 51 for a definition of the regions). Proportionately to other regions, there are more minorities in the Pacific, South Atlantic, and West South Central.

Figure 2: Minority Professionals by Region in US ARL University Libraries, FY 2009–2010

	New England	Middle Atlantic	East North Central	West North Central	South Atlantic	East South Central	West South Central	Mountain	Pacific	TOTAL	%
Race/Ethnicity Category											
Black	35	62	69	25	127	25	35	9	29	416	32%
Hispanic	23	41	31	11	38	5	41	20	43	253	20%
Asian	76	105	57	30	83	8	37	17	170	583	45%
AI/AN*	3	3	24	4	2		2	6		44	3%
Minority Total	137	211	181	70	250	38	115	52	242	1,296	100%
Minority Percent	10.60%	16.30%	14.00%	5.40%	19.30%	2.90%	8.90%	4.00%	18.70%		
Nonminority Total	1,177	1,257	1,371	537	1,224	371	592	445	841	7,815	100%
Nonminority Percent	15.10%	16.10%	17.50%	6.90%	15.70%	4.70%	7.60%	5.70%	10.80%		
Regional Percent Total staff	14.40%	16.10%	17.00%	6.70%	16.20%	4.50%	7.80%	5.50%	11.90%		
Proportional Minority Representation	-29.80%	1.24%	-20.00%	-21.74%	22.93%	-38.30%	17.11%	-29.82%	73.15%		

* American Indian/Alaskan Native

ARL recognizes the difficulties that the profession has in attracting a diverse workforce and continues to work actively in the development of workplace climates that embrace diversity. The ARL Diversity Program, through its Leadership and Career Development Program and the Initiative to Recruit a Diverse Workforce, emphasizes ARL's and its members' commitment to creating a diverse academic and research library community to better meet the new challenges of global competition and changing demographics. Further, the Diversity

Program focuses on issues surrounding work relationships in libraries while considering the impact of diversity on library services, interactions with library users, and the development of collections, at its homepage, http://www.arl.org/diversity/.

Women comprise 68.2% of the four racial/ethnic groups that comprise minority staff, as compared to 62.7% of Caucasian/Other staff in all US ARL university libraries. The overall gender balance in the 114 Canadian and US university libraries (including law and medical) is 35.9% male and 64.1% female. See Figure 2, above, and Figure 3, below, for more detail on race/ethnic and gender distribution.

Figure 3: Race/Ethnicity and Sex Distribution of Professional Staff in ARL University Libraries, FY 2009–2010

UNITED STATES					
	Men		**Women**		**Total**
	Number of Staff	**Percent of Total**	**Number of Staff**	**Percent of Total**	
Main	2,840	37.5%	4,725	62.5%	7,565
Medical	251	29.7%	595	70.3%	846
Law	239	33.9%	466	66.1%	705
Minority*	412	31.8%	884	68.2%	1,296
Non-minority	2,916	37.3%	4,899	62.7%	7,815
All	3,328	36.5%	5,783	63.5%	9,111
CANADA					
	Men		**Women**		**Total**
	Number of Staff	**Percent of Total**	**Number of Staff**	**Percent of Total**	
Main	308	32.5%	639	67.5%	947
Medical	11	10.8%	91	89.2%	102
Law	14	33.3%	28	66.7%	42
All	333	30.5%	758	69.5%	1,091
UNITED STATES AND CANADA (COMBINED)					
	Men		**Women**		**Total**
	Number of Staff	**Percent of Total**	**Number of Staff**	**Percent of Total**	
Main	3,148	37.0%	5,364	63.0%	8,512
Medical	262	27.6%	686	72.4%	948
Law	253	33.9%	494	66.1%	747
All	3,663	35.9%	6,544	64.1%	10,207

* Includes staff in medical and law libraries.

Note: There are five entries from a US institution that did not report their race/ethnicity; therefore, the totals will not aggregate to the sum needed for the US and Canadian sub-totals to equal the figure displayed in the combined total.

Gender data

Many readers of previous surveys have inquired about evidence of gender-based salary differentials in ARL libraries. Additionally, data on salary comparisons for directors also are frequently requested. 2009–2010 repeated a trend observed in 2008–2009, the average salary for female directors was slightly higher than that of their male counterparts (see Table 17); furthermore, the number of women in the top administrative library position continued to increase (68 female directors out of 114 total director positions reported; compared to 63 out of 111 in 2008–2009).

However, salaries for women have not yet met parity with that of men (see Table 17): in 2009–2010 (just as in 2008–2009) the overall salary for women was only 96.2% that of men for the 114 ARL university libraries (compared to 95.39% in 2007–2008). This suggests a slow, long-term trend towards closure of the gender gap in ARL libraries — in 1980–1981 women in ARL libraries made roughly 87% that of men.

Table 17 displays 27 job categories; females earn more than their male counterparts in just 10 of 27 categories listed. Table 18 provides average years of professional experience for many of the same staffing categories for which salary data are shown in Table 17, revealing that experience differentials may explain some differences within specific job categories. Women have more experience in all but three of the 10 job categories in which they average higher pay, but there are other categories in which women, on average, have more experience and less pay: Assistant Director, Functional Specialist, and Department Head — Other. Table 19 further reveals that the average salary for men is consistently higher than the average salary for women in nine of the ten experience cohorts, a pattern that is also repeated among minority librarians: the average salary for minority men is higher than that for minority women in eight of the ten experience cohorts (see Table 30).

There is a sense that the gender gap persists in academe in areas beyond the library and that a renewed commitment to resolve the problem is needed.[3] A variety of reasons have been offered as to why these trends persist, most notably the perception that work is peripheral in a woman's life and, consequently, female-dominated professions are undervalued. Librarianship is predominantly and persistently a woman's profession. The scarcity of men in the profession has been well documented in many studies — the largest percentage of men employed in ARL libraries was 38.2% in 1980–1981; since then men have consistently represented about 35% of the professional staff in ARL libraries.

The Functional Specialist Breakdown

In 2004, the ARL Statistics and Measurement Committee accepted a proposal from the ACRL Personnel Administrators and Staff Development Officers Discussion Group to break down the Functional Specialist category (FSPEC). The group's major concern was that so many different types of positions, with their varying job descriptions and salaries, were being labeled with the code FSPEC that data reported for the category were beginning to lose meaning. For each position that would have been labeled FSPEC in past years, the proposal offered ARL institutions two options: either use one of eight new codes to describe that position; or, if none of the eight new codes could adequately describe that position, use FSPEC. As seen in Figure 4, only 15.6% of Functional Specialists in all libraries did not use an alternative code, a slight decrease from 17% in 2008–2009. Of the positions that did use an alternate code, 63.2% were Archivists or Information Technology specialists.

---

[3] There are many instances citing the continuation of gender inequity in academia. See, for example: Denise K. Manger's articles in the *Chronicle of Higher Education*, "Faculty Salaries Increased 3.7% in 1999–2000" (14 April 2000: A20) and "Faculty Salaries are Up 3.6%, Double the Rate of Inflation" (23 April 1999: A16); D. W. Miller, "Salary Gap Between Male and Female Professors Grows Over the Years, Study Suggests," *Chronicle of Higher Education*, Today's News, 27 April 2000; and Yolanda Moses, "Salaries in Academe: The Gender Gap Persists," *Chronicle of Higher Education* 12 December 1997: A60.

Figure 4: Distribution of Functional Specialist Job Sub-Codes by Type of Library

Position	Main		Medical		Law		All	
	No.	Percent	No.	Percent	No.	Percent	No.	Percent
Archivists	489	23.2%	22	13.4%	6	11.1%	517	22.2%
Business Manager	140	6.6%	16	9.8%	1	1.9%	157	6.7%
Human Resources	90	4.3%	1	0.6%	0	0.0%	91	3.9%
IT, Systems	406	19.3%	36	22.0%	14	25.9%	456	19.6%
IT, Web Developer	153	7.3%	22	13.4%	7	13.0%	182	7.8%
IT, Programmer	289	13.7%	28	17.1%	0		317	13.6%
Media Specialist	102	4.8%	6	3.7%	4	7.4%	112	4.8%
Preservation	127	6.0%	3	1.8%	3	5.6%	133	5.7%
Other Functional Specialists	313	14.8%	30	18.3%	19	35.2%	362	15.6%
Total	**2,109**		**164**		**54**		**2,327**	

Figure 5, below, displays the average salaries of the subcategories by position and sex (law and medical libraries not included) in the same fashion as Table 17. The salaries in each of the sub-categories deviate widely from the combined Functional Specialist average salary of $63,897. Human resource specialists have the highest average of all subcategories, with an average salary of $71,840; media/multimedia specialists have the lowest average salary of $54,794.

Figure 5: Distribution of Functional Specialist Job Sub-Codes' Average Salaries by Sex

Position	Women		Men		Total	
	Salary	No.	Salary	No.	Salary	No.
Archivists	57,541	306	60,534	183	58,661	489
Business Manager	69,677	88	72,629	52	70,774	140
Human Resources	70,826	75	76,907	15	71,840	90
IT, Systems	65,346	142	64,944	264	65,085	406
IT, Web Developer	60,787	67	63,836	86	62,500	153
IT, Programmer	65,278	86	67,450	203	66,804	289
Media Specialist	55,199	45	54,474	57	54,794	102
Preservation	62,682	96	65,905	31	63,469	127
Other Functional Specialists	60,351	201	62,577	112	61,148	313
All Functional Specialists	**63,076**	**1,106**	**65,473**	**1,003**	**63,897**	**2,109**

In regards to the gender gap in ARL libraries explained in the previous section, it is worth noting that the average salaries of men are higher than those of women in seven out of the nine categories in Figure 5.

Institutional Characteristics and Salaries

A. Public and Private Institutions

The gap between salaries paid in private US ARL university libraries and those paid in publicly supported US university libraries decreased slightly; in 2008–2009 it was 7%, in 2009–2010 the difference was 6%, with an average of $4,120 more paid for a position in a private institution. Out of 27 job categories, only in four (Heads of Documents/Maps, Heads of Rare Books/Manuscripts, Heads of Computer Systems and Other: Over 14 years experience) did librarians in public institutions earn more than their peers employed in private institutions (see Table 21).

B. Library Size

Library size, as measured by the number of professional staff, is another significant determinant of salary. As a rule, the largest libraries pay the highest average salaries, not only overall, but for specific positions as well.[4] The largest libraries, those with more than 110 staff, reported the highest average salary, $72,765, compared to $71,620 for the libraries with between 75 and 110 staff (see Table 23). The smallest libraries (22 to 49 staff) had the third-highest average salary of the cohorts, followed by those libraries with 50 to 74 staff. The gap between the highest paying cohort and the lowest paying cohort remained unchanged, in 2009–2010 it was $4,901, a difference of 6.8% percent (the difference in 2008–2009 was $4,994, which was 7.2%).

C. Geographic Area

In 2009–2010, the highest average salaries were found in New England ($76,371) followed by the Pacific ($75,283) region with Canadian salaries ($73,363) coming in third (see Table 25). The reason for the drop in Canadian salaries relative to US institutions (highest in 2008–2009 at $82,295) was the change in the currency exchange rate: in the 2008–2009 salary survey it was 1.0101; for the 2009–2010 survey period it is 1.1667.[5] The East South Central region had the lowest average salary, with an average of $62,872.

D. Rank Structure

Rank structure provides a useful framework for examining professional salaries in ARL university libraries. Figure 6, below, displays average salary and years of experience in the three most commonly used rank structures. Readers should be aware that not all individuals have a rank that fits into the rank structure the library utilizes. Most commonly, directors may have no rank (or a rank outside the structure) and it is common for non-librarians included in the survey (business officers, personnel staff, computer specialists, liaisons, etc.) to be unranked, as well.

The pattern of relationships between rank and salary seen in past years continues: with higher rank associated with higher average years of experience and a correspondingly higher salary. Of the 8,512 librarians in ARL university member libraries, 6,082 occupy a rank within these three most commonly found ranking systems, and the largest number of professionals (3,223) occupy a position in a four-step rank structure.

---

[4] In 1995–1996, the largest cohort of libraries was determined based on staff over 124; in 1996–1998, over 120; in 1998–1999, over 115; and since 1999–2000, over 110. See Table 23.

[5] This is the average monthly noon exchange rate published in the Bank of Canada Review for the period July 2008–June 2009 and is used in converting figures that are shown effective as of 1 July 2009. This information can be accessed at: http://www.bankofcanada.ca/en/rates/exchange.html.

Figure 6: Average Salaries and Average Years of Experience of Library Professionals in Libraries with Three, Four, and Five Step Rank Structures, FY 2009–2010

	Three-Step		Four-Step		Five-Step	
	Salary	**Experience**	**Salary**	**Experience**	**Salary**	**Experience**
Librarian 1	54,708	8.7	51,078	7.2	53,339	8.7
Librarian 2	66,402	17.4	57,281	11.2	60,497	12.1
Librarian 3	84,896	25.4	70,677	20.5	70,433	17.8
Librarian 4			86,032	26.4	86,431	23.7
Librarian 5					102,257	30.0
No. of Staff	**1,883**		**3,223**		**976**	

INFLATION EFFECT

Tables 2 and 6 reveal changes in beginning professional and median salaries as reported by both university and nonuniversity research libraries as well as the US Bureau of Labor's Cost of Living Index (CPI-All Urban Consumers). Table 3 is similar to Table 2, but reports data only on US libraries. Table 4 shows trend data for Canadian libraries and compares them to the changes in the Canadian Consumer Price Index (Consumer Price Index for Canada, all-items, not seasonally adjusted). Tables 2, 3, and 4 include law and medical library staff in ARL university libraries. In contrast to 2007–2008, these tables indicate that the purchasing power of professionals (in both the United States and Canada) employed in ARL libraries outpaced inflation.

The median salary for US ARL university libraries in 2009 was $64,069, an increase of 0.6% over the 2008–2009 median salary of $63,673 (see Table 3). This modest salary increase compared favorably to the severe economic contraction of the same period, which saw the US CPI drop 2% (see Table 3).[6] Canadian salaries (when judged in Canadian dollars) were even more successful in surpassing inflation: while the Canadian CPI dropped -0.9%, median salaries in Canadian university libraries increased from $78,742 (Canadian) to $80,654 (Canadian) a rise of 2.4% (see Table 4).[7] However, the sharp difference in the exchange rates between 2008–2009 (1.0101 Canadian per US dollar) and 2009–2010 (1.1667 Canadian per US dollar), when judged in US currency, caused the Canadian median salary to drop from $77,954 in 2008–2009 to $69,130 — a decrease of 11.4% (see Table 4). This change in currency exchange rate is also responsible for the drop in overall (US and Canadian) median salary of ARL university librarians (see Table 2) from $64,823 (US dollars) in 2008–2009 to $64,560 (US dollars), which was a decrease of 0.5% despite the fact that both US and Canadian salaries increased modestly in 2009–2010 as stated above.

The median beginning salary (BPS) for university ARL librarians decreased during this survey's period: it was $44,000 (US) in 2008–2009 and dropped to $43,700 in 2009–2010 (a decrease of 0.7%) (see Table 2). Table 6 shows that nonuniversity librarians also experienced a decrease in their beginning salary, which was $48,108 in 2008–2009 and dropped to $47,554 in 2009–2010 (a difference of 1.2%). Table 6 also demonstrates that the median

---

[6] CPI data retrieved from the US Department of Labor, Bureau of Labor Statistics' *Consumer Price Index-All Urban Consumers (US All items, 1982-84=100 - CUUR0000SA0)* available online at http://www.bls.gov/data/.

[7] The source for Canadian CPI data is "Table 5: The Consumer Price Index for Canada (All-Items, Not Seasonally Adjusted, Historical Data)" published in *The Daily*, a Statistics Canada publication, available online at http://www.statcan.gc.ca/pub/62-001-x/2009010/t040-eng.htm.

salaries of ARL nonuniversity librarians remained virtually the same: $85,320 in 2008–2009, $85,229 in 2009–2010 — a decrease of 0.2%.

Readers are reminded that these data reflect only salaries and that there are other compensation issues which may have influenced the pattern of salaries in various institutions. In addition, a highly standardized structure for capturing data has been used, which may portray results in a way that cannot be fully representative of a local situation.

Martha Kyrillidou
Les Bland
Association of Research Libraries
April 1, 2010

SALARY LEVELS FOR STAFF IN ARL LIBRARIES

TABLES 1–4

TABLE 1: DISTRIBUTION BY SALARY LEVEL

Figures in columns headed by fiscal year show the number of filled professional positions. Columns headed by Cum. % show the percentage of all filled positions with salaries equal to or more than the beginning of each salary range. For example: in FY 2008–2009, 82.8% of all ARL university librarians earned more than $50,000, as did 96% of all ARL nonuniversity librarians.

Note: Canadian salaries are expressed in US dollars. Data includes medical and law libraries.

Salary Range	University Librarians				Nonuniversity Librarians			
	FY 2008–2009	Cum. %	FY 2009–2010	Cum. %	FY 2008–2009	Cum. %	FY 2009–2010	Cum. %
300,000 and above	7	0.1%	6	0.1%		0.0%		0.0%
250,000 - 299,999	10	0.2%	12	0.2%	1	0.0%	1	0.0%
200,000 - 249,999	36	0.5%	37	0.5%	2	0.1%	3	0.1%
175,000 - 199,999	55	1.1%	58	1.1%	3	0.2%	6	0.3%
150,000 - 174,999	91	2.0%	80	1.9%	112	3.1%	284	7.7%
140,000 - 149,999	55	2.5%	52	2.4%	197	8.4%	105	10.5%
130,000 - 139,999	87	3.4%	80	3.2%	115	11.5%	237	16.7%
120,000 - 129,999	124	4.6%	127	4.4%	251	18.2%	170	21.1%
110,000 - 119,999	229	6.8%	193	6.3%	237	24.5%	370	30.9%
100,000 - 109,999	369	10.5%	328	9.5%	373	34.4%	383	40.9%
95,000 - 99,999	296	13.4%	287	12.3%	241	40.9%	301	48.8%
90,000 - 94,999	296	16.3%	337	15.6%	312	49.2%	144	52.6%
85,000 - 89,999	413	20.4%	418	19.7%	195	54.4%	276	59.8%
80,000 - 84,999	568	26.0%	546	25.1%	244	60.9%	201	65.1%
79,000 - 79,999	110	27.1%	121	26.3%	60	62.5%	48	66.4%
78,000 - 78,999	119	28.2%	143	27.7%	59	64.1%	48	67.6%
76,000 - 77,999	250	30.7%	261	30.2%	60	65.7%	49	68.9%
74,000 - 75,999	322	33.9%	321	33.4%	130	69.2%	89	71.2%
72,000 - 73,999	299	36.8%	285	36.2%	88	71.5%	123	74.5%
70,000 - 71,999	301	39.8%	323	39.3%	92	74.0%	29	75.2%
68,000 - 69,999	410	43.8%	400	43.3%	114	77.0%	97	77.8%
66,000 - 67,999	351	47.3%	370	46.9%	40	78.1%	89	80.1%
64,000 - 65,999	473	51.9%	451	51.3%	123	81.4%	89	82.4%
62,000 - 63,999	365	55.5%	400	55.2%	83	83.6%	114	85.4%
60,000 - 61,999	523	60.7%	530	60.4%	114	86.6%	93	87.9%
58,000 - 59,999	420	64.8%	430	64.6%	159	90.8%	46	89.1%
56,000 - 57,999	466	69.4%	487	69.4%	46	92.1%	120	92.2%
54,000 - 55,999	441	73.8%	459	73.9%	34	93.0%	44	93.4%
52,000 - 53,999	475	78.4%	496	78.7%	65	94.7%	84	95.6%
50,000 - 51,999	441	82.8%	439	83.1%	47	96.0%	87	97.9%
48,000 - 49,999	417	86.9%	446	87.4%	66	97.7%	13	98.2%
46,000 - 47,999	361	90.5%	368	91.0%	30	98.5%	16	98.6%
44,000 - 45,999	321	93.6%	326	94.2%	7	98.7%	11	98.9%
42,000 - 43,999	217	95.8%	217	96.3%	24	99.4%	14	99.3%
40,000 - 41,999	182	97.6%	175	98.1%	3	99.4%	17	99.7%
38,000 - 39,999	109	98.6%	85	98.9%	9	99.7%	0	99.7%
36,000 - 37,999	60	99.2%	52	99.4%	0	99.7%	2	99.8%
34,000 - 35,999	43	99.6%	38	99.8%	0	99.7%	3	99.9%
less than 34,000	36	100.0%	23	100.0%	12	100.0%	5	100.0%
Total Positions	10,148		10,207		3,748		3,811	
Median Salary	**$64,828**		**$64,560**		**$80,320**		**$85,229**	

<h1 style="text-align:center">TABLE 2: SALARY TRENDS IN ARL UNIVERSITY LIBRARIES</h1>

Salary figures for the current year are displayed in the context of previous years and compared to the changes in the US Consumer Price Index (CPI) to show trends in the purchasing power of median and beginning professional salaries. Salary figures and CPI numbers have been converted to adjusted indexes, using July 1984 as the base. Actual CPI data retrieved from the US Department of Labor, Bureau of Labor Statistics' *Consumer Price Index-All Urban Consumers (US All items, 1982–1984=100 - CUUR0000SA0)* available online at http://www.bls.gov/data/.

Note: Canadian salaries are expressed in US dollars.

Fiscal Year	Number of Libraries	Total Staff	Median Salary[†]	BPS[‡] Median	Median Salary Index	BPS[‡] Index	Actual CPI[*]	Adjusted CPI
2009–2010	114	10,207	$64,560	$43,700	247.3	264.8	215.4	207.3
2008–2009	113	10,148	64,823	44,000	248.4	266.7	219.9	211.6
2007–2008	113	9,983	61,833	41,125	236.9	249.7	208.3	200.5
2006–2007	113	9,824	59,648	40,000	228.5	242.4	203.5	195.9
2005–2006	113	9,655	57,074	37,920	218.7	229.8	195.4	188.1
2004–2005	113	9,487	55,250	36,984	211.7	224.1	189.4	182.3
2003–2004	114	9,492	53,000	36,000	203.1	218.2	183.9	177.0
2002–2003	114	9,469	51,636	35,000	197.8	212.1	180.1	173.3
2001–2002	113	9,198	50,724	34,000	194.3	206.1	177.5	170.8
2000–2001	112	8,882	49,068	32,879	188.0	199.3	172.8	166.3
1999–2000	111	8,595	47,377	31,100	181.5	188.5	166.7	160.4
1998–1999	110	8,400	45,775	30,000	175.2	181.7	163.2	157.1
1997–1998	110	8,414	44,534	28,500	170.5	172.6	160.5	154.5
1996–1997	109	8,325	43,170	27,687	165.3	167.7	157.0	151.1
1995–1996	108	8,231	41,901	27,000	160.5	163.6	152.5	146.8
1994–1995	108	8,216	41,088	26,000	157.4	157.6	148.4	142.8
1993–1994	108	8,132	40,225	25,834	154.1	156.6	144.4	139.0
1992–1993	108	8,212	39,265	25,000	150.4	151.5	140.5	134.9
1991–1992	107	8,256	38,537	24,000	147.7	145.5	136.2	131.1
1990–1991	107	8,382	36,701	23,800	140.6	144.2	130.4	125.8
1989–1990	107	8,253	34,629	22,000	132.7	133.3	124.4	119.3
1988–1989	107	8,087	32,461	20,400	124.4	123.6	118.5	113.9
1987–1988	106	7,962	30,534	19,460	117.0	117.9	113.8	109.3
1986–1987	105	7,718	28,941	18,250	110.9	110.6	109.5	105.5
1985–1986	105	7,543	27,485	17,500	105.3	106.1	107.8	103.6
1984–1985	104	7,161	26,100	16,500	100.0	100.0	104.1	100.0

[*]Actual CPI figures have been revised from previous editions based upon changes published by the Bureau of Labor Statistics. These changes are minute, less than 0.3 in all cases.
[†] Includes medical and law libraries.
[‡] Beginning professional salary.

TABLE 3: SALARY TRENDS IN US ARL UNIVERSITY LIBRARIES

Salary figures for the current year are displayed in the context of previous years and compared to the changes in the US Consumer Price Index (CPI) to show trends in the purchasing power of median and beginning professional salaries. Salary figures and CPI numbers have been converted to adjusted indexes, using July 1984 as the base. Actual CPI data retrieved from the US Department of Labor, Bureau of Labor Statistics' *Consumer Price Index-All Urban Consumers (US All items, 1982–1984=100 - CUUR0000SA0)* available online at http://www. bls.gov/data/.

Fiscal Year	Number of Libraries	Total Staff	Median Salary[†]	Median Salary Change	Median Salary Index	Actual CPI[*]	Adjusted CPI	CPI Change
2009–2010	99	9,116	$64,069	0.6%	246.9	215.4	207.3	-2.0%
2008–2009	99	9,158	63,673	3.8	245.4	219.9	211.6	5.6
2007–2008	99	9,026	61,329	3.5	236.4	208.3	200.5	2.4
2006–2007	99	8,866	59,280	3.7	228.5	203.5	195.9	4.1
2005–2006	99	8,700	57,173	2.8	220.4	195.4	188.1	3.2
2004–2005	99	8,581	55,600	3.2	214.3	189.4	182.3	3.0
2003–2004	100	8,581	53,859	2.0	207.6	183.9	177.0	2.1
2002–2003	100	8,544	52,789	1.9	203.5	180.1	173.3	1.5
2001–2002	99	8,337	51,806	4.1	199.7	177.5	170.8	2.7
2000–2001	99	8,127	49,753	3.7	191.8	172.8	166.3	3.7
1999-2000	98	7,858	48,000	4.1	185.0	166.7	160.4	2.1
1998–1999	97	7,671	46,130	3.6	177.8	163.2	157.1	1.7
1997–1998	97	7,682	44,544	3.4	171.7	160.5	154.5	2.2
1996–1997	96	7,562	43,084	3.4	166.1	157.0	151.1	3.0
1995–1996	95	7,435	41,651	2.7	160.5	152.5	146.8	2.8
1994–1995	95	7,401	40,573	3.4	156.4	148.4	142.8	2.8
1993–1994	95	7,390	39,257	3.0	151.3	144.4	139.0	2.8
1992–1993	95	7,375	38,124	3.0	146.9	140.5	134.9	3.2
1991–1992	94	7,408	37,009	3.5	142.6	136.2	131.1	4.4
1990–1991	94	7,543	35,761	5.2	137.8	130.4	125.8	4.8
1989–1990	94	7,344	34,000	5.8	131.0	124.4	119.3	5.0
1988–1989	94	7,252	32,149	5.4	123.9	118.5	113.9	4.1
1987–1988	93	7,145	30,492	5.1	117.5	113.8	109.3	3.9
1986–1987	92	6,886	29,021	6.5	111.9	109.5	105.5	1.6
1985–1986	91	6,707	27,249	5.0	105.0	107.8	103.6	3.6
1984–1985	91	6,456	25,946	6.9	100.0	104.1	100.0	-

[*]Actual CPI figures have been revised from previous editions based upon changes published by the Bureau of Labor Statistics. These changes were caused by rounding; they are minute and are less than 0.3 in all cases.
[†] Includes medical and law libraries.

TABLE 4: SALARY TRENDS IN CANADIAN ARL UNIVERSITY LIBRARIES

Salary figures for the current year are displayed in the context of previous years. Canadian salaries are presented in both US $ and Canadian $ denominations and the annual exchange rate used in the salary surveys is also listed. Canadian salaries are also compared to the changes in the Canadian Consumer Price Index (CPI) to show trends in the purchasing power of median Canadian salaries. CPI number changes are based on July CPI figures. The source for Canadian CPI data is "Table 5: The Consumer Price Index for Canada" published in *The Daily*, a Statistics Canada publication, available online at http://www.statcan.gc.ca/pub/62-001-x/2009010/t040-eng.htm.

Fiscal Year	No. of Libs.	Total Staff	Median Salary in US $[†]	Median Salary Change[†]	Exchange Rate	Median Salary in Can. $	Median Salary Change	Can. CPI**	Can. CPI Change*
2009–2010	15	1,091	$69,130	-11.3%	1.1667	$80,654	2.4%	114.7	-0.9%
2008–2009	14	990	77,954	15.8	1.0101	78,742	3.3	115.8	3.4
2007–2008	14	957	67,331	6.7	1.1323	76,239	3.9	112.0	2.2
2006–2007	14	958	63,112	11.8	1.16289	73,392	4.0	109.6	2.3
2005–2006	14	955	56,474	7.1	1.24971	70,576	-0.3	107.1	2.0
2004–2005	14	906	52,707	16.3	1.34328	70,800	3.5	105.0	2.3
2003–2004	14	911	45,310	6.2	1.51023	68,429	2.3	102.6	2.1
2002–2003	14	925	42,657	-0.6	1.56878	66,919	2.6	100.5	2.1
2001–2002	14	861	42,928	-1.1	1.51919	65,215	2.1	98.4	2.7
2000–2001	13	755	43,394	5.0	1.47192	63,873	2.4	95.8	2.9
1999-2000	13	737	41,316	-3.8	1.5103	62,400	2.4	93.1	1.9
1998–1999	13	729	42,963	-2.7	1.4177	60,909	0.9	91.4	1.0
1997–1998	13	732	44,167	1.4	1.3663	60,346	1.7	90.5	1.7
1996–1997	13	764	43,569	0.9	1.3613	59,310	-0.4	89.0	1.3
1995–1996	13	796	43,173	-1.7	1.3794	59,554	1.3	87.9	2.6
1994–1995	13	815	43,919	-6.0	1.3381	58,768	0.7	85.7	0.1
1993–1994	13	816	46,744	-4.3	1.2488	58,374	2.9	85.6	1.7
1992–1993	13	837	48,820	2.7	1.1623	56,744	3.4	84.2	1.2
1991–1992	13	847	47,519	5.5	1.1547	54,870	3.6	83.2	6.0
1990–1991	13	839	45,023	15.1	1.1759	52,942	12.5	78.5	4.1
1989–1990	13	853	39,117	12.3	1.2026	47,042	5.3	75.4	5.3
1988–1989	13	837	34,826	11.7	1.2826	44,668	5.3	71.6	3.9
1987–1988	13	817	31,178	10.9	1.3602	42,408	9.1	68.9	4.6
1986–1987	13	831	28,123	-1.9	1.3817	38,858	1.2	65.9	4.1
1985–1986	13	829	28,666	1.1	1.3388	38,378	7.9	63.3	4.1
1984–1985	12	705	28,346	-0.8	1.2548	35,569	0.8	60.8	4.1
Average				3.8%			3.3%		

[†] Includes medical and law libraries.
* Canadian CPI change figures have been revised from previous editions based upon changes published by *The Daily* (Statistics Canada). These changes were caused by rounding; they are minute and are less than 0.3 in all cases.
** Actual Canadian CPI figures have been added to this table (not available in previous editions).

ARL NONUNIVERSITY LIBRARIES

TABLES 5–6

TABLE 5: MEDIAN AND BEGINNING PROFESSIONAL SALARIES IN ARL NONUNIVERSITY LIBRARIES

	No. of Staff	Median Salaries*		Beginning Salaries*	
		FY 2008–2009	FY 2009–2010	FY 2008–2009	FY 2009–2010
Boston Public Library	174	$63,736	$67,184	$39,782	$40,975
Canada Institute for Scientific and Technical Information * †	188	72,217	67,639	49,441	44,446
Center for Research Libraries†	34	42,348	50,799	33,878	33,878
Library of Congress †	2,633	96,791	101,416	48,108	50,408
National Agricultural Library †	93	79,060	82,845	48,108	50,408
Library & Archives Canada *	107	62,031	56,601	49,472	45,141
National Library of Medicine†	209	86,046	90,154	48,108	50,408
New York Public Library	258	59,963	63,696	39,295	42,638
New York State Library	57	58,849	64,305	47,556	49,968
Smithsonian Institution Libraries	58	81,394	85,281	49,712	52,089

* Canadian salaries are expressed in US dollars.
† See footnotes.

TABLE 6: SALARY TRENDS IN ARL NONUNIVERSITY LIBRARIES

Salary figures for the current year are displayed in the context of the previous years and compared to the changes in the Consumer Price Index (CPI) to show trends in the purchasing power of median and beginning professional salaries. Salary figures and CPI numbers have been converted to adjusted indexes, using July 1984 as the base. Actual CPI data retrieved from the US Department of Labor, Bureau of Labor Statistics' *Consumer Price Index-All Urban Consumers (US All items, 1982–1984=100 - CUUR0000SA0)* available online at http://www. bls.gov/data/.

Fiscal Year	Number of Libraries	Total Staff	Median Salary*	BPS[†] Median	Median Salary Index	BPS[†] Index	Actual CPI	Adjusted CPI
2009–2010	10	3,811	$85,229	$47,554	251.6	288.1	215.4	207.3
2008–2009	10	3,748	85,320	48,108	251.8	291.4	219.9	211.6
2007–2008	10	3,797	80,261	44,359	236.9	268.7	208.3	200.5
2006–2007	10	3,832	80,124	42,765	236.5	259.1	203.5	195.9
2005–2006	10	3,921	76,083	38,673	224.6	234.3	195.4	188.1
2004–2005	10	3,946	74,022	34,764	218.5	210.6	189.4	182.3
2003–2004	10	3,877	70,020	34,739	206.8	210.4	183.9	177.0
2002–2003	10	3,804	65,289	34,739	192.7	210.4	180.1	173.3
2001–2002	10	3,717	65,025	34,389	191.9	208.3	177.5	170.8
2000–2001	10	3,731	62,521	31,774	184.5	192.5	172.8	166.3
1999-2000	10	3,737	59,916	30,849	176.8	186.9	166.7	160.4
1998–1999	11	3,819	56,000	29,877	165.3	181.0	163.2	157.1
1997–1998	11	3,779	55,055	28,724	162.5	174.0	160.5	154.5
1996–1997	11	3,799	51,150	28,380	151.0	172.0	157.0	151.1
1995–1996	11	3,915	49,149	28,162	145.1	170.7	152.5	146.8
1994–1995	11	3,837	47,997	27,813	141.7	168.6	148.4	142.8
1993–1994	11	4,003	44,949	26,806	132.7	162.5	144.4	139.0
1992–1993	11	4,172	43,876	23,500	129.6	142.4	140.2	134.9
1991–1992	11	2,906	42,455	23,500	125.4	142.4	136.2	131.1
1990–1991	12	1,363	36,013	20,800	106.3	126.1	130.7	125.8
1989–1990	11	3,767	40,106	20,195	118.4	122.4	124.0	119.3
1988–1989	11	3,781	37,544	19,100	110.9	115.8	118.3	113.9
1987–1988	11	3,765	36,250	18,405	107.0	111.5	113.6	109.3
1986–1987	10	2,790	33,020	17,912	97.5	108.6	109.6	105.5
1985–1986	12	3,874	33,720	17,308	99.6	104.9	107.6	103.6
1984–1985	11	3,840	33,863	16,500	100.0	100.0	103.9	100.0

* Canadian salaries expressed in US dollars.
† Beginning professional salary.

ARL University Libraries

Tables 7–25

TABLE 7: FILLED POSITIONS; AVERAGE, MEDIAN, BEGINNING PROFESSIONAL SALARIES; AND AVERAGE YEARS OF EXPERIENCE IN ARL UNIVERSITY LIBRARIES, FY 2009–2010

Institution	Filled Positions FY 2010	Average Salaries FY 2009	Average Salaries FY 2010	Median Salaries FY 2009	Median Salaries FY 2010	Beginning Salaries FY 2009	Beginning Salaries FY 2010	Average Yrs. Exp. FY 2010
Alabama ‡	60	$58,655	$58,272	$52,205	$52,204	$42,000	$42,000	15.2
Alberta †‡	62	89,260	84,172	95,438	89,319	50,126	43,398	17.5
Arizona ‡	60	66,447	65,897	61,595	59,915	47,093	48,605	17.6
Arizona State ‡	58	63,110	66,091	61,000	65,071	43,000	43,000	18.8
Auburn ‡	45	60,231	58,382	55,290	53,705	44,720	44,720	15.1
Boston University ‡	59	59,236	57,615	55,200	56,600	42,300	43,700	16.5
Boston College ‡	61	69,672	69,739	67,184	67,280	42,300	42,300	19.1
Brigham Young ‡	111	63,925	66,005	62,400	63,950	48,000	51,000	18.2
British Columbia †‡	94	79,910	73,023	80,769	70,005	53,021	47,429	15.0
Brown ‡	74	67,804	65,880	63,854	61,549	39,500	39,500	20.5
Calgary‡	57	N/A	81,275	N/A	76,749	N/A	49,713	18.3
California, Berkeley ‡	113	82,952	83,853	80,374	82,524	46,164	47,087	18.2
California, Davis ‡	43	79,652	81,135	82,637	88,488	46,164	46,164	21.1
California, Irvine	56	76,045	76,645	75,708	75,708	46,164	46,164	15.4
California, Los Angeles ‡	147	75,812	78,189	73,799	75,708	46,164	46,164	16.1
California, Riverside ‡	45	74,166	77,661	74,400	75,708	47,087	47,087	21.0
California, San Diego ‡	93	76,016	77,158	75,708	75,708	46,164	46,164	16.4
California, Santa Barbara ‡	61	71,466	71,378	68,892	68,892	46,164	46,164	17.0
Case Western Reserve ‡	41	57,972	58,788	54,389	55,227	35,000	35,000	15.3
Chicago ‡	72	74,480	76,254	70,290	72,329	48,204	48,204	19.3
Cincinnati ‡	52	66,847	65,445	61,332	61,879	39,000	40,000	20.9
Colorado ‡	41	66,826	67,523	64,388	64,573	44,000	44,000	16.4
Colorado State	46	68,355	68,311	65,300	65,300	45,400	45,000	17.6
Columbia	185	72,352	72,939	64,265	64,385	51,500	51,500	15.8
Connecticut ‡	58	79,855	82,083	78,680	78,079	48,000	48,000	18.3
Cornell ‡	103	69,564	71,548	63,600	64,239	47,000	47,000	16.1
Dartmouth ‡	48	72,539	72,208	69,536	67,933	42,500	45,500	17.6
Delaware‡	58	72,792	75,703	71,037	73,353	43,600	43,600	18.2
Duke ‡	122	63,058	64,870	58,583	60,000	44,000	45,000	16.8
Emory ‡	73	69,025	68,747	63,653	63,068	41,500	42,000	15.1
Florida ‡	68	58,974	60,450	55,045	56,388	42,000	42,000	15.4
Florida State ‡	48	49,803	54,858	47,000	49,805	42,000	42,000	13.9
George Washington	39	70,759	74,353	65,328	67,143	47,000	47,000	15.6
Georgetown ‡	53	69,739	69,227	63,538	63,538	45,000	45,000	21.4
Georgia‡	74	57,628	56,544	51,005	50,000	38,000	38,000	16.0
Georgia Tech	42	60,944	63,526	56,270	58,016	42,000	44,000	16.7
Guelph †‡	50	77,319	69,113	71,928	66,902	57,242	51,169	17.7
Harvard ‡	454	78,019	77,319	70,900	70,720	48,800	48,800	15.8
Hawaii ‡	83	67,491	66,721	67,391	66,225	42,649	42,660	16.0
Houston ‡	44	63,512	61,669	62,480	56,563	42,000	43,000	14.1
Howard ‡	30	53,741	43,547	53,440	43,010	36,000	38,000	18.9
Illinois, Chicago ‡	47	61,206	62,208	56,457	56,555	47,000	47,000	17.6
Illinois, Urbana	151	67,213	66,755	62,036	61,645	46,000	46,000	14.4
Indiana ‡	80	63,786	63,870	60,011	59,331	40,400	40,400	19.1
Iowa ‡	71	63,196	62,529	56,796	55,573	41,000	41,000	17.7
Iowa State ‡	53	61,863	63,217	59,887	61,664	43,000	43,000	19.7
Johns Hopkins ‡	75	67,265	68,926	63,702	65,690	50,026	50,026	17.4
Kansas ‡	86	61,056	60,877	56,200	54,806	49,000	51,000	15.5
Kent State ‡	59	57,317	63,997	53,777	60,301	43,389	55,367	15.7
Kentucky ‡	65	60,909	60,966	59,697	59,839	41,000	41,000	21.1
Laval †	62	68,511	61,963	69,901	62,474	47,613	42,468	14.4
Louisiana State	50	51,839	50,821	47,715	46,462	38,000	38,000	13.5
Louisville ‡	31	61,851	59,483	56,845	55,884	37,000	37,000	18.2
McGill †	65	73,148	63,797	67,233	57,834	49,500	42,856	16.7
McMaster †‡	48	78,776	61,608	78,858	62,508	44,771	40,128	16.8
Manitoba †‡	41	89,270	81,855	93,351	85,771	46,970	41,845	22.8
Maryland	84	67,924	68,874	66,419	66,603	42,000	40,000	19.9
Massachusetts ‡	59	70,508	69,882	72,263	72,263	42,155	42,155	16.4
MIT ‡	94	75,733	74,430	70,900	70,959	51,000	51,750	16.0

TABLE 7: FILLED POSITIONS; AVERAGE, MEDIAN, BEGINNING PROFESSIONAL SALARIES; AND AVERAGE YEARS OF EXPERIENCE IN ARL UNIVERSITY LIBRARIES, FY 2009–2010

Institution	Filled Positions FY 2010	Average Salaries FY 2009	Average Salaries FY 2010	Median Salaries FY 2009	Median Salaries FY 2010	Beginning Salaries FY 2009	Beginning Salaries FY 2010	Average Yrs. Exp. FY 2010
Miami ‡	49	69,165	68,278	64,935	61,728	45,000	45,000	16.5
Michigan ‡	122	70,031	67,767	65,564	63,717	42,000	42,000	16.0
Michigan State ‡	67	63,867	68,894	60,000	65,850	47,000	47,000	16.4
Minnesota	107	67,975	66,794	65,446	63,557	40,000	42,000	16.4
Missouri ‡	39	55,264	59,914	48,854	55,964	40,000	40,000	19.4
Montreal †‡	92	69,342	62,740	66,631	59,349	41,738	36,968	15.1
Nebraska	47	65,751	65,057	57,671	57,472	50,000	50,000	19.4
New Mexico ‡	43	78,591	72,938	76,307	68,853	40,000	40,000	20.8
New York University ‡	53	78,920	79,018	70,769	69,989	52,000	52,000	18.4
North Carolina	99	67,177	67,637	63,750	63,712	44,000	44,000	17.9
North Carolina State ‡	84	70,667	73,019	64,895	65,000	49,000	50,000	11.0
Northwestern ‡	88	66,328	67,873	62,847	63,429	42,000	43,000	17.0
Notre Dame ‡	63	68,224	69,492	65,738	66,508	40,000	41,200	18.3
Ohio University ‡	47	54,210	55,522	48,170	48,787	41,500	41,000	13.6
Ohio State ‡	122	57,439	59,476	52,432	54,450	43,000	46,000	14.4
Oklahoma	41	54,228	55,853	52,228	53,742	42,000	42,000	14.4
Oklahoma State ‡	65	56,703	56,580	53,640	52,657	36,000	38,000	16.8
Oregon ‡	57	56,965	59,782	53,792	55,973	40,000	40,000	16.2
Pennsylvania ‡	105	65,914	65,997	61,122	61,850	42,500	43,500	16.1
Pennsylvania State ‡	145	69,421	67,897	65,556	64,224	42,436	42,436	19.3
Pittsburgh ‡	65	66,544	66,551	59,984	60,711	34,000	34,000	18.8
Princeton ‡	122	77,939	79,015	72,150	73,799	50,000	63,200	21.0
Purdue ‡	65	66,957	65,573	61,000	60,513	45,000	47,000	18.5
Queen's †	35	88,107	80,504	89,828	83,438	49,500	44,227	20.0
Rice	59	61,433	62,215	55,450	55,833	38,300	37,200	15.9
Rochester ‡	74	55,965	55,837	52,540	53,000	38,168	38,168	14.8
Rutgers ‡	84	88,899	89,058	92,106	91,751	47,390	49,286	21.7
Saskatchewan †‡	40	85,401	76,307	85,977	78,850	49,600	45,197	17.4
South Carolina ‡	53	53,670	53,658	49,838	49,838	34,000	34,000	16.6
Southern California ‡	103	73,788	74,479	66,944	67,650	48,500	48,500	18.4
Southern Illinois	38	57,003	58,264	49,117	52,536	43,000	44,000	14.0
SUNY Albany ‡	62	67,251	60,964	59,704	58,822	38,500	39,000	16.5
SUNY Buffalo ‡	76	69,982	72,916	66,684	69,048	45,000	45,000	20.3
SUNY Stony Brook	26	75,948	79,837	73,259	75,457	44,000	42,000	22.2
Syracuse ‡	54	65,441	65,847	61,493	60,648	N/A	None	18.2
Temple ‡	40	66,114	66,849	56,020	58,140	42,744	44,044	19.1
Tennessee ‡	42	70,344	69,380	67,823	66,307	44,000	44,000	18.5
Texas ‡	120	66,554	66,882	58,958	59,260	45,000	46,000	16.7
Texas A&M ‡	134	59,250	62,441	54,156	55,704	47,000	47,500	16.0
Texas Tech ‡	61	60,494	60,690	55,036	57,135	45,000	45,000	11.8
Toronto †‡	143	90,829	78,211	91,773	75,194	51,381	44,484	15.7
Tulane	33	62,896	60,534	60,000	56,325	40,000	40,000	16.5
Utah‡	54	61,119	61,470	57,250	56,312	44,000	44,000	19.0
Vanderbilt ‡	62	59,810	58,991	54,666	54,655	40,000	40,500	17.4
Virginia ‡	74	69,246	67,988	60,450	60,000	44,000	44,000	15.9
Virginia Tech	36	65,516	63,148	62,556	58,540	41,000	40,000	16.7
Washington ‡	117	66,517	66,476	60,312	59,934	42,600	42,600	19.7
Washington State ‡	44	59,820	62,755	56,482	58,172	38,500	38,500	18.7
Washington U.-St. Louis ‡	63	59,497	59,037	54,468	53,740	40,000	40,000	16.1
Waterloo †‡	36	77,432	70,230	78,311	70,260	49,090	44,402	17.9
Wayne State ‡	67	54,962	61,261	50,031	54,705	40,500	40,500	15.0
Western Ontario †‡	68	68,168	59,073	63,872	55,725	46,906	40,610	13.2
Wisconsin ‡	157	60,304	61,856	57,808	58,654	40,526	40,526	16.5
Yale ‡	213	82,622	81,088	76,974	76,300	50,500	50,500	18.9
York †‡	54	95,755	82,297	88,458	77,321	48,510	41,999	17.2

Directors are included in figures for average years of experience and filled positions, but not in either the average or median salary statistics. Excludes medical and law libraries. See Tables 35 and 42 for statistics related to medical and law library salaries.
† Canadian salaries are expressed in US dollars. ‡ See Footnotes.

TABLE 8: BEGINNING PROFESSIONAL SALARIES IN ARL UNIVERSITY LIBRARIES
RANK ORDER TABLE, FY 2008–2009

Rank	Institution	Salary	Rank	Institution	Salary
1	Guelph	57,242	58	Delaware	43,600
2	British Columbia	53,021	59	Kent State	43,389
3	New York	52,000	60	Arizona State	43,000
4	Columbia	51,500	60	Iowa State	43,000
5	Toronto	51,381	60	Ohio State	43,000
6	MIT	51,000	60	Southern Illinois	43,000
7	Yale	50,500	64	Temple	42,744
8	Alberta	50,126	65	Hawaii	42,649
9	Johns Hopkins	50,026	66	Washington	42,600
10	Nebraska	50,000	67	Dartmouth	42,500
10	Princeton	50,000	67	Pennsylvania	42,500
12	Saskatchewan	49,600	69	Pennsylvania State	42,436
13	McGill	49,500	70	Boston University	42,300
13	Queen's	49,500	70	Boston College	42,300
15	Waterloo	49,090	72	Massachusetts	42,155
16	Kansas	49,000	73	Alabama	42,000
16	North Carolina State	49,000	73	Florida	42,000
18	Harvard	48,800	73	Florida State	42,000
19	York	48,510	73	Georgia Tech	42,000
20	Southern California	48,500	73	Houston	42,000
21	Chicago	48,204	73	Maryland	42,000
22	Brigham Young	48,000	73	Michigan	42,000
22	Connecticut	48,000	73	Northwestern	42,000
24	Laval	47,613	73	Oklahoma	42,000
25	Rutgers	47,390	82	Montreal	41,738
26	Arizona	47,093	83	Emory	41,500
27	Calif. Riverside	47,087	83	Ohio	41,500
28	Cornell	47,000	85	Iowa	41,000
28	George Washington	47,000	85	Kentucky	41,000
28	Illinois, Chicago	47,000	85	Virginia Tech	41,000
28	Michigan State	47,000	88	Wisconsin	40,526
28	Texas A&M	47,000	89	Wayne State	40,500
33	Manitoba	46,970	90	Indiana	40,400
34	Western Ontario	46,906	91	Minnesota	40,000
35	Calif. Berkeley	46,164	91	Missouri	40,000
35	Calif. Davis	46,164	91	New Mexico	40,000
35	Calif. Irvine	46,164	91	Notre Dame	40,000
35	Calif. Los Angeles	46,164	91	Oregon	40,000
35	Calif. San Diego	46,164	91	Tulane	40,000
35	Calif. Santa Barbara	46,164	91	Vanderbilt	40,000
41	Illinois, Urbana	46,000	91	Washington-St. Louis	40,000
42	Colorado State	45,400	99	Brown	39,500
43	Georgetown	45,000	100	Cincinnati	39,000
43	Miami	45,000	101	SUNY Albany	38,500
43	Purdue	45,000	101	Washington State	38,500
43	SUNY Buffalo	45,000	103	Rice	38,300
43	Texas	45,000	104	Rochester	38,168
43	Texas Tech	45,000	105	Georgia	38,000
49	McMaster	44,771	105	Louisiana State	38,000
50	Auburn	44,720	107	Louisville	37,000
51	Colorado	44,000	108	Howard	36,000
51	Duke	44,000	108	Oklahoma State	36,000
51	North Carolina	44,000	110	Case Western Reserve	35,000
51	SUNY Stony Brook	44,000	111	Pittsburgh	34,000
51	Tennessee	44,000	111	South Carolina	34,000
51	Utah	44,000	113	Syracuse	N/A
51	Virginia	44,000			

Reprinted from *ARL Annual Salary Survey 2008–2009*. Beginning salary figures represent officially designated base, not necessarily salaries of actual incumbents.

Excludes medical and law libraries. See Tables 36 and 43 for statistics related to medical and law library salaries.

Canadian salaries are expressed in US dollars.

TABLE 9: BEGINNING PROFESSIONAL SALARIES IN ARL UNIVERSITY LIBRARIES
RANK ORDER TABLE, FY 2009–2010

Rank	Institution	Salary	Rank	Institution	Salary
1	Princeton	63,200	58	Delaware	43,600
2	Kent State	55,367	59	Pennsylvania	43,500
3	New York	52,000	60	Alberta	43,398
4	MIT	51,750	61	Arizona State	43,000
5	Columbia	51,500	61	Houston	43,000
6	Guelph	51,169	61	Iowa State	43,000
7	Brigham Young	51,000	61	Northwestern	43,000
7	Kansas	51,000	65	McGill	42,856
9	Yale	50,500	66	Hawaii	42,660
10	Johns Hopkins	50,026	67	Washington	42,600
11	Nebraska	50,000	68	Laval	42,468
11	North Carolina State	50,000	69	Pennsylvania State	42,436
13	Calgary	49,713	70	Boston College	42,300
14	Rutgers	49,286	71	Massachusetts	42,155
15	Harvard	48,800	72	Alabama	42,000
16	Arizona	48,605	72	Emory	42,000
17	Southern California	48,500	72	Florida	42,000
18	Chicago	48,204	72	Florida State	42,000
19	Connecticut	48,000	72	Michigan	42,000
20	Texas A&M	47,500	72	Minnesota	42,000
21	British Columbia	47,429	72	Oklahoma	42,000
22	Calif. Berkeley	47,087	72	SUNY Stony Brook	42,000
22	Calif. Riverside	47,087	80	York	41,999
24	Cornell	47,000	81	Manitoba	41,845
24	George Washington	47,000	82	Notre Dame	41,200
24	Illinois, Chicago	47,000	83	Iowa	41,000
24	Michigan State	47,000	83	Kentucky	41,000
24	Purdue	47,000	83	Ohio	41,000
29	Calif. Davis	46,164	86	Western Ontario	40,610
29	Calif. Irvine	46,164	87	Wisconsin	40,526
29	Calif. Los Angeles	46,164	88	Vanderbilt	40,500
29	Calif. San Diego	46,164	88	Wayne State	40,500
29	Calif. Santa Barbara	46,164	90	Indiana	40,400
34	Illinois, Urbana	46,000	91	McMaster	40,128
34	Ohio State	46,000	92	Cincinnati	40,000
34	Texas	46,000	92	Maryland	40,000
37	Dartmouth	45,500	92	Missouri	40,000
38	Saskatchewan	45,197	92	New Mexico	40,000
39	Colorado State	45,000	92	Oregon	40,000
39	Duke	45,000	92	Tulane	40,000
39	Georgetown	45,000	92	Virginia Tech	40,000
39	Miami	45,000	92	Washington-St. Louis	40,000
39	SUNY Buffalo	45,000	100	Brown	39,500
39	Texas Tech	45,000	101	SUNY Albany	39,000
45	Auburn	44,720	102	Washington State	38,500
46	Toronto	44,484	103	Rochester	38,168
47	Waterloo	44,402	104	Georgia	38,000
48	Queen's	44,227	104	Howard	38,000
49	Temple	44,044	104	Louisiana State	38,000
50	Colorado	44,000	104	Oklahoma State	38,000
50	Georgia Tech	44,000	108	Rice	37,200
50	North Carolina	44,000	109	Louisville	37,000
50	Southern Illinois	44,000	110	Montreal	36,968
50	Tennessee	44,000	111	Case Western Reserve	35,000
50	Utah	44,000	112	Pittsburgh	34,000
50	Virginia	44,000	112	South Carolina	34,000
57	Boston University	43,700	N/A	Syracuse	None

Beginning salary figures represent officially designated base, not necessarily salaries of actual incumbents.
Excludes medical and law libraries. See Tables 36 and 43 for statistics related to medical and law library salaries.
Canadian salaries are expressed in US dollars.

TABLE 10: MEDIAN PROFESSIONAL SALARIES IN ARL UNIVERSITY LIBRARIES
RANK ORDER TABLE, FY 2008–2009

Rank	Institution	Salary	Rank	Institution	Salary
1	Alberta	95,438	58	Virginia Tech	62,556
2	Manitoba	93,351	59	Houston	62,480
3	Rutgers	92,106	60	Brigham Young	62,400
4	Toronto	91,773	61	Illinois, Urbana	62,036
5	Queen's	89,828	62	Arizona	61,595
6	York	88,458	63	Syracuse	61,493
7	Saskatchewan	85,977	64	Cincinnati	61,332
8	California, Davis	82,637	65	Pennsylvania	61,122
9	British Columbia	80,769	66	Arizona State	61,000
10	California, Berkeley	80,374	66	Purdue	61,000
11	McMaster	78,858	68	Virginia	60,450
12	Connecticut	78,680	69	Washington	60,312
13	Waterloo	78,311	70	Indiana	60,011
14	Yale	76,974	71	Michigan State	60,000
15	New Mexico	76,307	71	Tulane	60,000
16	California, Irvine	75,708	73	Pittsburgh	59,984
16	California, San Diego	75,708	74	Iowa State	59,887
18	California, Riverside	74,400	75	SUNY Albany	59,704
19	California, Los Angeles	73,799	76	Kentucky	59,697
20	SUNY Stony Brook	73,259	77	Texas	58,958
21	Massachusetts	72,263	78	Duke	58,583
22	Princeton	72,150	79	Wisconsin	57,808
23	Guelph	71,928	80	Nebraska	57,671
24	Delaware	71,037	81	Utah	57,250
25	Harvard	70,900	82	Louisville	56,845
25	MIT	70,900	83	Iowa	56,796
27	New York University	70,769	84	Washington State	56,482
28	Chicago	70,290	85	Illinois, Chicago	56,457
29	Laval	69,901	86	Georgia Tech	56,270
30	Dartmouth	69,536	87	Kansas	56,200
31	California, Santa Barbara	68,892	88	Temple	56,020
32	Tennessee	67,823	89	Rice	55,450
33	Hawaii	67,391	90	Auburn	55,290
34	McGill	67,233	91	Boston University	55,200
35	Boston College	67,184	92	Florida	55,045
36	Southern California	66,944	93	Texas Tech	55,036
37	SUNY Buffalo	66,684	94	Vanderbilt	54,666
38	Montreal	66,631	95	Washington U.-St. Louis	54,468
39	Maryland	66,419	96	Case Western Reserve	54,389
40	Notre Dame	65,738	97	Texas A&M	54,156
41	Michigan	65,564	98	Oregon	53,792
42	Pennsylvania State	65,556	99	Kent State	53,777
43	Minnesota	65,446	100	Oklahoma State	53,640
44	George Washington	65,328	101	Howard	53,440
45	Colorado State	65,300	102	Rochester	52,540
46	Miami	64,935	103	Ohio State	52,432
47	North Carolina State	64,895	104	Oklahoma	52,228
48	Colorado	64,388	105	Alabama	52,205
49	Columbia	64,265	106	Georgia	51,005
50	Western Ontario	63,872	107	Wayne State	50,031
51	Brown	63,854	108	South Carolina	49,838
52	North Carolina	63,750	109	Southern Illinois	49,117
53	Johns Hopkins	63,702	110	Missouri	48,854
54	Emory	63,653	111	Ohio University	48,170
55	Cornell	63,600	112	Louisiana State	47,715
56	Georgetown	63,538	113	Florida State	47,000
57	Northwestern	62,847			

Reprinted from *ARL Annual Salary Survey 2008–2009*. Salaries of directors are not included in the calculation of medians. Excludes medical and law libraries. See Tables 37 and 44 for statistics related to medical and law library salaries. Canadian salaries are expressed in US dollars.

Table 11: Median Professional Salaries in ARL University Libraries
Rank Order Table, FY 2009–2010

Rank	Institution	Salary	Rank	Institution	Salary
1	Rutgers	91,751	58	Pennsylvania	61,850
2	Alberta	89,319	59	Miami	61,728
3	California, Davis	88,488	60	Iowa State	61,664
4	Manitoba	85,771	61	Illinois, Urbana	61,645
5	Queen's	83,438	62	Brown	61,549
6	California, Berkeley	82,524	63	Pittsburgh	60,711
7	Saskatchewan	78,850	64	Syracuse	60,648
8	Connecticut	78,079	65	Purdue	60,513
9	York	77,321	66	Kent State	60,301
10	Calgary	76,749	67	Duke	60,000
11	Yale	76,300	67	Virginia	60,000
12	California, Irvine	75,708	69	Washington	59,934
12	California, Los Angeles	75,708	70	Arizona	59,915
12	California, Riverside	75,708	71	Kentucky	59,839
12	California, San Diego	75,708	72	Montreal	59,349
16	SUNY Stony Brook	75,457	73	Indiana	59,331
17	Toronto	75,194	74	Texas	59,260
18	Princeton	73,799	75	SUNY Albany	58,822
19	Delaware	73,353	76	Wisconsin	58,654
20	Chicago	72,329	77	Virginia Tech	58,540
21	Massachusetts	72,263	78	Washington State	58,172
22	MIT	70,959	79	Temple	58,140
23	Harvard	70,720	80	Georgia Tech	58,016
24	Waterloo	70,260	81	McGill	57,834
25	British Columbia	70,005	82	Nebraska	57,472
26	New York University	69,989	83	Texas Tech	57,135
27	SUNY Buffalo	69,048	84	Boston University	56,600
28	California, Santa Barbara	68,892	85	Houston	56,563
29	New Mexico	68,853	86	Illinois, Chicago	56,555
30	Dartmouth	67,933	87	Florida	56,388
31	Southern California	67,650	88	Tulane	56,325
32	Boston College	67,280	89	Utah	56,312
33	George Washington	67,143	90	Oregon	55,973
34	Guelph	66,902	91	Missouri	55,964
35	Maryland	66,603	92	Louisville	55,884
36	Notre Dame	66,508	93	Rice	55,833
37	Tennessee	66,307	94	Western Ontario	55,725
38	Hawaii	66,225	95	Texas A&M	55,704
39	Michigan State	65,850	96	Iowa	55,573
40	Johns Hopkins	65,690	97	Case Western Reserve	55,227
41	Colorado State	65,300	98	Kansas	54,806
42	Arizona State	65,071	99	Wayne State	54,705
43	North Carolina State	65,000	100	Vanderbilt	54,655
44	Colorado	64,573	101	Ohio State	54,450
45	Columbia	64,385	102	Oklahoma	53,742
46	Cornell	64,239	103	Washington U.-St. Louis	53,740
47	Pennsylvania State	64,224	104	Auburn	53,705
48	Brigham Young	63,950	105	Rochester	53,000
49	Michigan	63,717	106	Oklahoma State	52,657
50	North Carolina	63,712	107	Southern Illinois	52,536
51	Minnesota	63,557	108	Alabama	52,204
52	Georgetown	63,538	109	Georgia	50,000
53	Northwestern	63,429	110	South Carolina	49,838
54	Emory	63,068	111	Florida State	49,805
55	McMaster	62,508	112	Ohio University	48,787
56	Laval	62,474	113	Louisiana State	46,462
57	Cincinnati	61,879	114	Howard	43,010

Salaries of directors are not included in the calculation of medians.
Excludes medical and law libraries. See Tables 37 and 44 for statistics related to medical and law library salaries.
Canadian salaries are expressed in US dollars.

TABLE 12: AVERAGE PROFESSIONAL SALARIES IN ARL UNIVERSITY LIBRARIES
RANK ORDER TABLE, FY 2008–2009

Rank	Institution	Salary	Rank	Institution	Salary
1	York	95,755	58	North Carolina	67,177
2	Toronto	90,829	59	Purdue	66,957
3	Manitoba	89,270	60	Cincinnati	66,847
4	Alberta	89,260	61	Colorado	66,826
5	Rutgers	88,899	62	Texas	66,554
6	Queen's	88,107	63	Pittsburgh	66,544
7	Saskatchewan	85,401	64	Washington	66,517
8	California, Berkeley	82,952	65	Arizona	66,447
9	Yale	82,622	66	Northwestern	66,328
10	British Columbia	79,910	67	Temple	66,114
11	Connecticut	79,855	68	Pennsylvania	65,914
12	California, Davis	79,652	69	Nebraska	65,751
13	New York University	78,920	70	Virginia Tech	65,516
14	McMaster	78,776	71	Syracuse	65,441
15	New Mexico	78,591	72	Brigham Young	63,925
16	Harvard	78,019	73	Michigan State	63,867
17	Princeton	77,939	74	Indiana	63,786
18	Waterloo	77,432	75	Houston	63,512
19	Guelph	77,319	76	Iowa	63,196
20	California, Irvine	76,045	77	Arizona State	63,110
21	California, San Diego	76,016	78	Duke	63,058
22	SUNY Stony Brook	75,948	79	Tulane	62,896
23	California, Los Angeles	75,812	80	Iowa State	61,863
24	MIT	75,733	81	Louisville	61,851
25	Chicago	74,480	82	Rice	61,433
26	California, Riverside	74,166	83	Illinois, Chicago	61,206
27	Southern California	73,788	84	Utah	61,119
28	McGill	73,148	85	Kansas	61,056
29	Delaware	72,792	86	Georgia Tech	60,944
30	Dartmouth	72,539	87	Kentucky	60,909
31	Columbia	72,352	88	Texas Tech	60,494
32	California, Santa Barbara	71,466	89	Wisconsin	60,304
33	George Washington	70,759	90	Auburn	60,231
34	North Carolina State	70,667	91	Washington State	59,820
35	Massachusetts	70,508	92	Vanderbilt	59,810
36	Tennessee	70,344	93	Washington U.-St. Louis	59,497
37	Michigan	70,031	94	Texas A&M	59,250
38	SUNY Buffalo	69,982	95	Boston University	59,236
39	Georgetown	69,739	96	Florida	58,974
40	Boston College	69,672	97	Alabama	58,655
41	Cornell	69,564	98	Case Western Reserve	57,972
42	Pennsylvania State	69,421	99	Georgia	57,628
43	Montreal	69,342	100	Ohio State	57,439
44	Virginia	69,246	101	Kent State	57,317
45	Miami	69,165	102	Southern Illinois	57,003
46	Emory	69,025	103	Oregon	56,965
47	Laval	68,511	104	Oklahoma State	56,703
48	Colorado State	68,355	105	Rochester	55,965
49	Notre Dame	68,224	106	Missouri	55,264
50	Western Ontario	68,168	107	Wayne State	54,962
51	Minnesota	67,975	108	Oklahoma	54,228
52	Maryland	67,924	109	Ohio University	54,210
53	Brown	67,804	110	Howard	53,741
54	Hawaii	67,491	111	South Carolina	53,670
55	Johns Hopkins	67,265	112	Louisiana State	51,839
56	SUNY Albany	67,251	113	Florida State	49,803
57	Illinois, Urbana	67,213			

Reprinted from *ARL Annual Salary Survey 2008–2009*. Salaries of directors are not included in the calculation of medians.
Excludes medical and law libraries. See Tables 38 and 45 for statistics related to medical and law library salaries.
Canadian salaries are expressed in US dollars.

TABLE 13: AVERAGE PROFESSIONAL SALARIES IN ARL UNIVERSITY LIBRARIES
RANK ORDER TABLE, FY 2009–2010

Rank	Institution	Salary	Rank	Institution	Salary
1	Rutgers	89,058	58	Pittsburgh	66,551
2	Alberta	84,172	59	Washington	66,476
3	California, Berkeley	83,853	60	Arizona State	66,091
4	York	82,297	61	Brigham Young	66,005
5	Connecticut	82,083	62	Pennsylvania	65,997
6	Manitoba	81,855	63	Arizona	65,897
7	Calgary	81,275	64	Brown	65,880
8	California, Davis	81,135	65	Syracuse	65,847
9	Yale	81,088	66	Purdue	65,573
10	Queen`s	80,504	67	Cincinnati	65,445
11	SUNY Stony Brook	79,837	68	Nebraska	65,057
12	New York University	79,018	69	Duke	64,870
13	Princeton	79,015	70	Kent State	63,997
14	Toronto	78,211	71	Indiana	63,870
15	California, Los Angeles	78,189	72	McGill	63,797
16	California, Riverside	77,661	73	Georgia Tech	63,526
17	Harvard	77,319	74	Iowa State	63,217
18	California, San Diego	77,158	75	Virginia Tech	63,148
19	California, Irvine	76,645	76	Washington State	62,755
20	Saskatchewan	76,307	77	Montreal	62,740
21	Chicago	76,254	78	Iowa	62,529
22	Delaware	75,703	79	Texas A&M	62,441
23	Southern California	74,479	80	Rice	62,215
24	MIT	74,430	81	Illinois, Chicago	62,208
25	George Washington	74,353	82	Laval	61,963
26	British Columbia	73,023	83	Wisconsin	61,856
27	North Carolina State	73,019	84	Houston	61,669
28	Columbia	72,939	85	McMaster	61,608
29	New Mexico	72,938	86	Utah	61,470
30	SUNY Buffalo	72,916	87	Wayne State	61,261
31	Dartmouth	72,208	88	Kentucky	60,966
32	Cornell	71,548	89	SUNY Albany	60,964
33	California, Santa Barbara	71,378	90	Kansas	60,877
34	Waterloo	70,230	91	Texas Tech	60,690
35	Massachusetts	69,882	92	Tulane	60,534
36	Boston College	69,739	93	Florida	60,450
37	Notre Dame	69,492	94	Missouri	59,914
38	Tennessee	69,380	95	Oregon	59,782
39	Georgetown	69,227	96	Louisville	59,483
40	Guelph	69,113	97	Ohio State	59,476
41	Johns Hopkins	68,926	98	Western Ontario	59,073
42	Michigan State	68,894	99	Washington U.-St. Louis	59,037
43	Maryland	68,874	100	Vanderbilt	58,991
44	Emory	68,747	101	Case Western Reserve	58,788
45	Colorado State	68,311	102	Auburn	58,382
46	Miami	68,278	103	Alabama	58,272
47	Virginia	67,988	104	Southern Illinois	58,264
48	Pennsylvania State	67,897	105	Boston University	57,615
49	Northwestern	67,873	106	Oklahoma State	56,580
50	Michigan	67,767	107	Georgia	56,544
51	North Carolina	67,637	108	Oklahoma	55,853
52	Colorado	67,523	109	Rochester	55,837
53	Texas	66,882	110	Ohio University	55,522
54	Temple	66,849	111	Florida State	54,858
55	Minnesota	66,794	112	South Carolina	53,658
56	Illinois, Urbana	66,755	113	Louisiana State	50,821
57	Hawaii	66,721	114	Howard	43,547

Salaries of directors are not included in the calculation of medians.

Excludes medical and law libraries. See Tables 38 and 45 for statistics related to medical and law library salaries.

Canadian salaries are expressed in US dollars.

TABLE 14: AVERAGE, MEDIAN, AND BEGINNING PROFESSIONAL SALARIES IN ARL UNIVERSITY LIBRARIES
SUMMARY OF RANKINGS, FY 2006–2007 to 2009–2010

Institution	Average Salaries				Median Salaries				Beginning Salaries			
FY	2007	2008	2009	2010	2007	2008	2009	2010	2007	2008	2009	2010
Alabama	98	92	97	103	101	96	105	108	84	74	73	72
Alberta	17	11	4	2	3	2	1	2	43	38	8	60
Arizona	38	56	65	63	55	56	62	70	21	7	26	16
Arizona State	69	59	77	60	66	41	66	42	23	34	60	61
Auburn	77	75	90	102	52	63	90	104	15	25	50	45
Boston University	104	106	40	105	97	100	91	84	112	62	70	57
Boston College	36	35	95	36	36	31	35	32	58	57	70	70
Brigham Young	68	70	72	61	59	55	60	48	17	14	22	7
British Columbia	41	26	10	26	32	22	9	25	20	15	2	21
Brown	53	47	53	64	61	42	51	62	84	94	99	100
Calgary*	N/A	N/A	N/A	7	N/A	N/A	N/A	10	N/A	N/A	N/A	13
California, Berkeley	2	3	8	3	6	5	10	6	64	69	35	22
California, Davis	18	15	12	8	8	3	8	3	64	69	35	29
California, Irvine	8	20	20	19	5	13	16	12	64	69	35	29
California, Los Angeles	5	10	23	15	7	12	19	12	64	69	35	29
California, Riverside	29	28	26	16	22	24	18	12	26	41	27	22
California, San Diego	11	14	21	18	10	13	16	12	44	69	35	29
California, Santa Barbara	19	23	32	33	21	27	31	28	64	43	35	29
Case Western Reserve	94	96	98	101	88	90	96	97	104	108	110	111
Chicago	14	18	25	21	18	23	28	20	9	12	21	18
Cincinnati	49	49	60	67	53	47	64	57	84	94	100	92
Colorado	71	46	61	52	63	49	48	44	37	58	51	50
Colorado State	55	68	48	45	41	53	45	41	45	29	42	39
Columbia	12	21	31	28	26	46	49	45	2	1	4	5
Connecticut	7	7	11	5	15	9	12	8	5	5	22	19
Cornell	28	33	41	32	43	40	55	46	22	16	28	24
Dartmouth	20	19	30	31	20	16	30	30	75	74	67	37
Delaware	26	29	29	22	28	34	24	19	64	28	58	58
Duke	75	76	78	69	76	81	78	67	93	34	51	39
Emory	60	57	46	44	54	51	54	54	84	94	83	72
Florida	93	100	96	93	93	98	92	87	27	44	73	72
Florida State	113	113	113	111	113	111	113	111	37	44	73	72
George Washington	40	54	33	25	62	62	44	33	27	44	28	24
Georgetown	43	40	39	39	51	48	56	52	11	16	43	39
Georgia	99	97	99	107	104	106	106	109	111	108	105	104
Georgia Tech	72	90	86	73	85	86	86	80	17	44	73	50
Guelph	56	69	19	40	56	66	23	34	80	90	1	6
Harvard	15	16	16	17	24	26	25	23	9	8	18	15
Hawaii	51	74	54	57	40	54	33	38	74	42	65	66
Houston	88	99	75	84	89	108	59	85	64	74	73	61
Howard	109	108	110	114	108	93	101	114	103	107	108	104
Illinois, Chicago	83	89	83	81	86	84	85	86	27	9	28	24

TABLE 14: AVERAGE, MEDIAN, AND BEGINNING PROFESSIONAL SALARIES IN ARL UNIVERSITY LIBRARIES
SUMMARY OF RANKINGS, FY 2006–2007 to 2009–2010

Institution	Average Salaries				Median Salaries				Beginning Salaries			
FY	2007	2008	2009	2010	2007	2008	2009	2010	2007	2008	2009	2010
Illinois, Urbana	54	62	57	56	71	68	61	61	23	26	41	34
Indiana	65	60	74	71	64	60	70	73	92	74	90	90
Iowa	67	65	76	78	83	79	83	96	45	74	85	83
Iowa State	76	82	80	74	72	75	74	60	37	39	60	61
Johns Hopkins	44	44	55	41	46	57	53	40	7	4	9	10
Kansas	86	86	85	90	78	82	87	98	45	74	16	7
Kent State	96	101	101	70	94	92	99	66	1	31	59	2
Kentucky	91	85	87	88	81	71	76	71	81	91	85	83
Laval	97	84	47	82	73	39	29	56	94	68	24	68
Louisiana State	112	112	112	113	112	113	112	113	99	94	105	104
Louisville	48	51	81	96	27	43	82	92	99	100	107	109
McGill	39	43	28	72	17	32	34	81	59	65	13	65
McMaster	64	37	14	85	38	20	11	55	96	89	49	91
Manitoba	9	5	3	6	4	4	2	4	71	55	33	81
Maryland	61	55	52	43	50	44	39	35	45	44	73	92
Massachusetts	25	27	35	35	11	19	21	21	60	63	72	71
MIT	24	25	24	24	29	29	25	22	11	5	6	4
Miami	42	52	45	46	65	58	46	59	36	16	43	39
Michigan	35	41	37	50	45	36	41	49	45	58	73	72
Michigan State	59	71	73	42	47	76	71	39	6	9	28	24
Minnesota	37	42	51	55	39	35	43	51	75	74	91	72
Missouri	105	95	106	94	102	104	110	91	108	91	91	92
Montreal	87	78	43	77	80	69	38	72	107	104	82	110
Nebraska	78	73	69	68	87	87	80	82	41	16	10	11
New Mexico	13	9	15	29	9	8	15	29	45	74	91	92
New York	10	4	13	12	31	21	27	26	2	2	3	3
North Carolina	47	34	58	51	44	37	52	50	27	44	51	50
North Carolina State	27	30	34	27	49	45	47	43	8	9	16	11
Northwestern	50	50	66	49	42	50	57	53	84	86	73	61
Notre Dame	32	38	49	37	30	28	40	36	83	74	91	82
Ohio University	111	111	100	110	111	112	111	112	104	105	83	83
Ohio State	85	98	109	97	79	95	103	101	41	54	60	34
Oklahoma	110	107	108	108	110	103	104	102	45	74	73	72
Oklahoma State	101	104	104	106	100	105	100	106	99	105	108	104
Oregon	107	103	103	95	103	102	98	90	104	108	91	92
Pennsylvania	52	66	68	62	48	64	65	58	27	39	67	59
Pennsylvania State	34	39	42	48	37	38	42	47	45	56	69	69
Pittsburgh	62	61	63	58	69	65	73	63	108	111	111	112
Princeton	16	13	17	13	23	18	22	18	45	16	10	1
Purdue	63	48	59	66	82	72	66	65	23	29	43	24
Queen's	23	17	6	10	14	11	5	5	73	64	13	48

TABLE 14: AVERAGE, MEDIAN, AND BEGINNING PROFESSIONAL SALARIES IN ARL UNIVERSITY LIBRARIES
SUMMARY OF RANKINGS, FY 2006–2007 to 2009–2010

Institution	Average Salaries				Median Salaries				Beginning Salaries			
FY	**2007**	**2008**	**2009**	**2010**	**2007**	**2008**	**2009**	**2010**	**2007**	**2008**	**2009**	**2010**
Rice	82	72	82	80	92	83	89	93	98	85	103	108
Rochester	102	102	105	109	99	101	102	105	95	103	104	103
Rutgers	1	1	5	1	1	1	3	1	16	13	25	14
Saskatchewan	31	12	7	20	25	10	7	7	102	53	12	38
South Carolina	108	110	111	112	106	109	108	110	108	111	111	112
Southern California	21	22	27	23	33	33	36	31	11	16	20	17
Southern Illinois	100	105	102	104	107	107	109	107	61	58	60	50
SUNY Albany	80	77	56	89	68	77	75	75	72	94	101	101
SUNY Buffalo	81	58	38	30	84	52	37	27	11	16	43	39
SUNY Stony Brook	22	24	22	11	19	25	20	16	27	34	51	72
Syracuse	58	53	71	65	74	67	63	64	113	N/A	113	N/A
Temple	46	45	67	54	57	78	88	79	75	86	64	49
Tennessee	45	32	36	38	34	30	32	37	45	44	51	50
Texas	57	64	62	53	67	73	77	74	17	16	43	34
Texas A&M	92	79	94	79	96	85	97	95	27	27	28	20
Texas Tech	106	81	88	91	105	94	93	83	75	16	43	39
Toronto	4	8	2	14	2	6	4	17	34	33	5	46
Tulane	73	87	79	92	60	80	71	88	84	100	91	92
Utah	90	80	84	86	91	88	81	89	45	44	51	50
Vanderbilt	89	94	92	100	95	97	94	100	75	86	91	88
Virginia	33	36	44	47	35	58	68	67	35	34	51	50
Virginia Tech	74	67	70	75	70	61	58	77	84	91	85	92
Washington	70	63	64	59	75	70	69	69	45	58	66	67
Washington State	79	91	91	76	77	89	84	78	81	94	101	102
Washington U.-St. Louis	84	93	93	99	90	99	95	103	84	100	91	92
Waterloo	30	31	18	34	16	17	13	24	63	52	15	47
Wayne State	103	109	107	87	109	110	107	99	45	67	89	88
Western Ontario	95	88	50	98	98	91	50	94	40	65	34	86
Wisconsin	66	83	89	83	58	74	79	76	62	84	88	87
Yale	3	6	9	9	13	15	14	11	4	3	7	9
York	6	2	1	4	12	7	6	9	97	32	19	80

Excludes medical and law libraries.

* Calgary became a member in FY 2010.

PAGE INTENTIONALLY LEFT BLANK.

Table 15: Distribution of Professional Staff in ARL University Libraries by Salary and Position, FY 2009–2010

Salary Intervals	Number of Staff								Percentage at Each Level[†]							
	Dir.	Assoc. Dir.	Asst. Dir.	Branch Head	Subj. Spec.	Func. Spec.	Dept. Head	Other Prof.	Dir.	Assoc. Dir.	Asst. Dir.	Branch Head	Subj. Spec.	Func. Spec.	Dept. Head	Other Prof.
More than 300,000	5								4%							
250,000 – 299,999	9							1	8%							0%
200,000 – 250,000	30	2	2	1			1		26%	1%	1%	0%			0%	
175,000 – 199,999	29	8	8						25%	3%	5%					
150,000 – 174,999	26	15	1	2	1		2	1	23%	5%	1%	0%	0%		0%	0%
140,000 – 149,999	4	18		3	2		6	1	4%	6%		1%	0%		0%	0%
130,000 – 139,999	7	36	8	3	3		4	1	6%	11%	5%	1%	0%		0%	0%
120,000 – 129,999	4	52	18	6	7		11	9	4%	16%	11%	1%	0%		1%	0%
110,000 – 119,999		53	22	16	11	15	29	10		17%	13%	3%	1%	1%	2%	1%
100,000 – 109,999		71	24	34	33	21	79	21		22%	14%	7%	2%	2%	6%	1%
95,000 – 99,999		18	21	26	40	32	63	44		6%	12%	5%	2%	3%	5%	2%
90,000 – 94,999		17	16	40	49	35	85	37		5%	9%	8%	2%	3%	6%	1%
85,000 – 89,999		7	11	37	78	40	122	68		2%	6%	8%	4%	4%	9%	2%
80,000 – 84,999		8	8	48	102	63	160	94		3%	5%	10%	5%	6%	12%	3%
79,000 – 79,999		1	2	8	24	14	30	25		0%	1%	2%	1%	1%	2%	1%
78,000 – 78,999		1	2	9	31	12	38	24		0%	1%	2%	1%	1%	3%	2%
76,000 – 77,999		1	3	16	53	36	61	48		0%	2%	3%	3%	3%	4%	3%
74,000 – 75,999		1	5	26	62	43	47	77		0%	3%	5%	3%	4%	3%	3%
72,000 – 73,999		2	2	20	62	31	58	57		1%	1%	4%	3%	3%	4%	2%
70,000 – 71,999			6	23	67	35	57	75			4%	5%	3%	3%	4%	3%
68,000 – 69,999			1	33	77	54	59	111			1%	7%	4%	5%	4%	4%
66,000 – 67,999			1	17	76	52	60	105			1%	3%	4%	5%	4%	4%
64,000 – 65,999		1	3	20	97	58	64	131		0%	2%	4%	4%	5%	5%	5%
62,000 – 63,999			1	18	78	65	42	121			1%	4%	4%	6%	3%	4%
60,000 – 61,999		2		17	120	68	55	171		1%		3%	6%	6%	4%	6%
58,000 – 59,999		1		10	101	45	40	155		0%		2%	5%	4%	3%	5%
56,000 – 57,999		1	1	10	102	61	39	179		0%	1%	2%	5%	5%	3%	6%
54,000 – 55,999			2	10	114	41	30	182			1%	2%	5%	4%	2%	6%
52,000 – 53,999			2	10	128	61	21	193			1%	2%	6%	5%	2%	7%
50,000 – 51,999				4	109	49	21	183				1%	5%	4%	2%	6%
48,000 – 49,999				5	119	62	13	183				1%	6%	5%	1%	6%
46,000 – 47,999				5	112	43	22	146				1%	5%	4%	2%	5%
44,000 – 45,999				6	82	41	11	124				1%	4%	4%	1%	4%
42,000 – 43,999				1	50	35	9	89				0%	2%	3%	1%	3%
40,000 – 41,999				2	55	14	7	71				0%	3%	1%	1%	3%
38,000 – 39,999				1	25	1	3	40				0%	1%	0%	0%	1%
36,000 – 37,999					18	3	3	22					1%	0%	0%	1%
34,000 – 35,999					16		4	15					1%		0%	1%
less than 34,000					5	3	2	12					0%	0%	0%	0%
TOTAL	114	316	170	487	2,109	1,133	1,358	2,825	100%	100%	100%	100%	100%	100%	100%	100%

Excludes medical and law libraries.

† A "0" percentage indicates less than one-half of one percent.

Table 16: Distribution of Professional Staff in ARL University Libraries by Salary, Sex, and Position, FY 2009–2010

Salary Intervals	Women								Men							
	Dir.	Assoc. Dir.	Asst. Dir.	Branch Head	Subj. Spec.	Func. Spec.	Dept. Head	Other Prof.	Dir.	Assoc. Dir.	Asst. Dir.	Branch Head	Subj. Spec.	Func. Spec.	Dept. Head	Other Prof.
More than 300,000	1								4							
250,000 - 299,999	7							1	2							
200,000 - 250,000	20	2	2						10	3	2	1			1	
175,000 - 199,999	18	5	5						11	6	5					
150,000 - 174,999	16	9	3		1		1		10	6	1	2			1	
140,000 - 149,999	1	12		1	2		2		3	15	5	2			4	1
130,000 - 139,999	3	21	3		2		3		4	23	10	3	1		1	1
120,000 - 129,999	2	29	8	3	5		6	8	2	19	10	3	2		5	1
110,000 - 119,999		34	12	10	7	6	20	7		28	11	6	4	9	9	3
100,000 - 109,999		43	13	25	16	15	46	17		5	8	9	17	6	33	4
95,000 - 99,999		13	13	16	14	18	34	32		8	4	10	26	14	29	12
90,000 - 94,999		9	12	24	19	15	55	20		3	5	16	30	20	30	17
85,000 - 89,999		4	6	26	28	25	71	49		3	2	11	50	15	51	19
80,000 - 84,999		5	6	31	49	41	105	69				17	53	22	55	25
79,000 - 79,999		1	1	5	8	8	18	21		1	1	3	16	6	12	4
78,000 - 78,999				4	18	7	23	20		1	2	5	13	5	15	4
76,000 - 77,999			3	12	27	23	40	28			3	4	26	13	21	20
74,000 - 75,999		1	2	16	36	24	28	57				10	26	19	19	20
72,000 - 73,999		2	2	16	29	22	39	43				4	33	9	19	14
70,000 - 71,999			6	15	32	18	41	47				8	35	17	16	28
68,000 - 69,999			1	24	43	29	36	76				9	34	25	23	35
66,000 - 67,999			1	12	36	32	44	73				5	40	20	16	32
64,000 - 65,999		1	2	13	56	38	33	96			1	7	41	20	31	35
62,000 - 63,999			1	13	43	39	27	89				5	35	26	15	32
60,000 - 61,999				13	59	42	37	124				4	61	26	18	47
58,000 - 59,999		1	1	3	54	32	24	106		2		7	47	13	16	49
56,000 - 57,999		1		7	57	33	24	124				3	45	28	15	55
54,000 - 55,999			1	7	63	28	18	121			1	3	51	13	12	61
52,000 - 53,999			1	10	67	48	11	143			1		61	13	10	50
50,000 - 51,999				4	63	33	18	125					46	16	3	58
48,000 - 49,999				1	57	42	9	137				4	62	20	4	46
46,000 - 47,999				2	69	27	16	98				3	43	16	6	48
44,000 - 45,999				5	49	31	9	84				1	33	10	2	40
42,000 - 43,999					27	27	6	67				1	23	8	3	22
40,000 - 41,999				2	28	12	6	58					27	2	1	13
38,000 - 39,999					16			32				1	9	1	3	8
36,000 - 37,999					15	1	2	13					3	2	1	9
34,000 - 35,999					9	1	2	14					7	2	2	1
less than 34,000					2			9					3		2	3
TOTAL	68	193	98	320	1,106	717	854	2,008	46	123	72	167	1,003	416	504	817

Excludes medical and law libraries.

Position	WOMEN		MEN		TOTAL	
	Salary	**No.**	**Salary**	**No.**	**Salary**	**No.**
Director	$197,433	68	$196,188	46	$196,930	114
Associate Director	117,708	193	116,845	123	117,372	316
Assistant Director	97,331	98	109,862	72	102,639	170
Head, Branch	78,079	320	82,727	167	79,673	487
Functional Specialist	62,070	1,106	64,299	1,003	63,130	2,109
Subject Specialist	64,332	717	67,459	416	65,480	1,133
Dept. Head:						
Acquisitions	74,986	79	70,942	33	73,794	112
Reference	77,320	78	80,958	30	78,331	108
Cataloging	74,317	109	74,251	40	74,299	149
Serials	75,123	21	69,354	9	73,392	30
Documents/Maps	68,333	36	70,020	23	68,990	59
Circulation	72,934	56	64,168	27	70,082	83
Rare Books/Manuscripts	80,587	40	83,992	50	82,479	90
Computer Systems	92,577	26	88,277	47	89,809	73
Other	76,631	409	78,638	245	77,382	654
Reference:						
Over 14 years experience	68,883	403	66,505	173	68,169	576
10 to 14 years experience	60,293	157	60,397	55	60,320	212
5 to 9 years experience	55,217	215	55,692	91	55,358	306
Under 5 years experience	48,558	195	48,739	59	48,600	254
Cataloging:						
Over 14 years experience	65,088	269	66,199	132	65,454	401
10 to 14 years experience	57,127	77	61,197	29	58,240	106
5 to 9 years experience	54,661	93	55,275	48	54,870	141
Under 5 years experience	49,693	81	48,978	31	49,496	112
Other:						
Over 14 years experience	68,142	221	68,260	78	68,173	299
10 to 14 years experience	61,221	88	59,435	35	60,713	123
5 to 9 years experience	55,932	95	58,224	36	56,562	131
Under 5 years experience	49,709	114	51,033	50	50,112	164
All Positions	**$69,277**	**5,364**	**$71,953**	**3,148**	**$70,266**	**8,512**

Canadian salaries are expressed in US dollars. See Table 32 for salaries of Canadian librarians expressed in Canadian dollars.
Excludes medical and law libraries. See Tables 39 and 46 for salaries in medical and law libraries.

Table 18: Number and Average Years of Experience of ARL University Librarians by Position and Sex, FY 2009–2010

Position	Women Years	Women No.	Men Years	Men No.	Total Years	Total No.
Director	33.3	68	32.5	46	33.0	114
Associate Director	26.7	193	23.8	123	25.6	316
Assistant Director	24.5	98	24.2	72	24.4	170
Head, Branch	21.6	320	22.9	167	22.0	487
Functional Specialist	13.9	1,106	13.4	1,003	13.6	2,109
Subject Specialist	16.1	717	17.0	416	16.4	1,133
Dept. Head:						
Acquisitions	21.5	79	16.8	33	20.2	112
Reference	20.0	78	21.1	30	20.3	108
Cataloging	22.2	109	21.0	40	21.8	149
Serials	21.0	21	20.2	9	20.8	30
Documents/Maps	19.8	36	21.4	23	20.4	59
Circulation	20.0	56	16.1	27	18.8	83
Rare Books/Manuscripts	21.5	40	23.9	50	22.8	90
Computer Systems	20.3	26	19.3	47	19.7	73
Other	20.6	409	19.3	245	20.1	654
Public Services	13.3	221	12.3	89	13.0	310
Technical Services	15.6	139	14.9	49	15.4	188
Administrative Services	15.2	158	13.4	61	14.7	219
Reference	14.6	970	15.1	378	14.8	1,348
Cataloger	17.0	520	17.9	240	17.3	760
All Positions	**17.1**	**5,364**	**16.9**	**3,148**	**17.0**	**8,512**

Includes Canadian libraries. See Table 33 for comparable figures in Canadian libraries only.
Excludes medical and law libraries. See Tables 40 and 47 for comparable figures in medical and law libraries.

Table 19: Number and Average Salaries of ARL University Librarians by Years of Experience and Sex, FY 2009–2010

Experience	WOMEN		MEN		TOTAL		% OF
	Salary	No.	Salary	No.	Salary	No.	TOTAL
0 – 3 years	$48,872	623	$50,893	339	$49,584	962	11%
4 – 7 years	54,555	701	56,165	409	55,148	1,110	13%
8 – 11 years	60,758	750	63,540	489	61,856	1,239	15%
12 – 15 years	66,656	583	68,728	369	67,459	952	11%
16 – 19 years	70,357	534	74,583	319	71,938	853	10%
20 – 23 years	74,484	543	77,753	312	75,677	855	10%
24 – 27 years	79,661	481	82,459	243	80,600	724	9%
28 – 31 years	82,859	415	87,795	277	84,835	692	8%
32 – 35 years	90,399	368	96,132	217	92,526	585	7%
over 35 years	94,251	366	95,301	174	94,589	540	6%
All Positions	**$69,277**	**5,364**	**$71,953**	**3,148**	**$70,266**	**8,512**	**100%**

Canadian salaries are expressed in US dollars. See Table 34 for salaries in Canadian dollars.
Excludes medical and law libraries. See Tables 41 and 48 for salaries in medical and law libraries.

TABLE 20: AVERAGE SALARIES OF ARL UNIVERSITY LIBRARIANS BY POSITION AND YEARS OF EXPERIENCE, FY 2009–2010

YEARS OF EXPERIENCE

Position	0–3 Years	4–7 Years	8–11 Years	12–15 Years	16–19 Years	20–23 Years	24–27 Years	28–31 Years	32–35 Years	over 35 Years
Director	.	.	‡	‡	‡	$182,450	$198,845	$187,198	$207,134	$197,328
Associate Director	.	$89,779	$94,637	$109,198	$112,860	117,047	118,438	117,846	125,564	128,467
Assistant Director	‡	74,889	86,504	92,812	106,585	99,764	102,438	108,287	113,008	108,485
Head, Branch	55,278	60,093	69,604	73,140	76,598	79,844	82,535	83,296	93,374	93,233
Functional Specialist	49,342	55,379	60,710	65,871	67,981	70,085	76,758	74,924	80,648	78,977
Subject Specialist	48,916	54,141	61,378	66,598	67,656	72,741	72,169	76,115	80,103	82,448
Dept. Head:										
Acquisitions	56,586	63,563	66,512	66,425	73,909	76,592	75,786	82,244	81,153	92,066
Reference	‡	64,000	74,170	76,861	79,697	73,044	81,603	91,631	89,163	92,183
Cataloging	49,023	60,128	60,371	70,042	72,881	75,463	79,962	76,135	92,692	77,783
Serials	.	‡	61,165	‡	81,999	76,177	‡	‡	‡	‡
Documents/Maps	52,291	57,222	‡	64,981	68,866	73,413	71,402	76,173	77,584	82,953
Circulation	52,719	61,263	56,359	71,724	76,537	73,111	70,005	96,536	78,554	80,336
Rare Books/Manuscripts	‡	‡	71,046	73,313	79,376	75,029	90,934	85,405	95,998	93,685
Computer Systems	78,463	‡	90,190	86,149	92,053	83,125	90,276	99,212	102,070	.
Other	57,134	61,728	66,308	74,892	80,257	80,329	80,760	83,378	87,193	88,544
Public Services	48,514	51,863	55,746	57,325	62,277	59,502	63,425	67,742	64,886	69,142
Technical Services	48,193	53,903	57,906	57,508	64,747	64,402	62,513	65,401	77,344	75,299
Administrative Services	52,854	54,107	67,214	65,018	71,724	70,141	89,064	73,861	84,562	91,478
Reference	48,021	52,716	57,733	61,609	61,798	68,597	69,395	70,484	71,515	76,840
Cataloger	49,127	53,345	57,235	58,673	62,175	64,635	65,119	66,984	67,167	69,653
All Positions:										
Average Salary	$49,584	$55,148	$61,856	6$7,459	$71,938	$75,677	$80,600	$84,835	$92,526	$94,589
No. of Positions	962	1,110	1,239	952	853	855	724	692	585	540

Years of experience reflect total professional experience. Canadian salaries are expressed in US dollars. Excludes medical and law libraries.
‡ Salary data are not published when fewer than four individuals are involved.
. No positions reported in this category.

Table 21: Number and Average Salaries of ARL University Librarians by Position and Type of Institution, FY 2009–2010

Position	Canadian (15) Salary	No.	Private (31) Salary	No.	Public (68) Salary	No.	Total (114) Salary	No.
Director	$151,500	15	$233,154	31	$190,438	68	$196,930	114
Associate Director	109,191	40	127,387	96	113,848	180	117,372	316
Assistant Director	91,609	19	108,281	67	100,633	84	102,639	170
Head, Branch	86,859	60	83,934	132	76,304	295	79,673	487
Functional Specialist	65,785	180	66,631	781	60,332	1,148	63,130	2,109
Subject Specialist	65,527	123	66,563	396	64,772	614	65,480	1,133
Dept. Head:								
Acquisitions	83,456	15	74,788	28	71,291	69	73,794	112
Reference	72,514	15	81,465	41	77,538	52	78,331	108
Cataloging	80,090	11	77,153	56	71,573	82	74,299	149
Serials	78,717	4	73,339	11	72,011	15	73,392	30
Documents/Maps	83,961	8	65,169	14	67,199	37	68,990	59
Circulation	69,888	14	73,250	18	69,018	51	70,082	83
Rare Books/Manuscripts	83,843	8	80,276	30	83,539	52	82,479	90
Computer Systems	82,756	7	88,599	23	91,604	43	89,809	73
Other	80,848	67	79,580	201	75,637	386	77,382	654
Reference:								
Over 14 years experience	80,653	83	66,413	150	65,916	343	68,169	576
10 to 14 years experience	70,692	29	59,948	61	58,041	122	60,320	212
5 to 9 years experience	61,424	71	57,477	67	51,949	168	55,358	306
Under 5 years experience	54,104	61	49,291	48	46,056	145	48,600	254
Cataloging:								
Over 14 years experience	73,160	37	66,179	165	63,420	199	65,454	401
10 to 14 years experience	57,874	10	60,295	47	56,344	49	58,240	106
5 to 9 years experience	63,124	9	58,906	64	49,979	68	54,870	141
Under 5 years experience	53,444	10	52,198	48	46,362	54	49,496	112
Other:								
Over 14 years experience	77,347	17	65,366	115	69,172	167	68,173	299
10 to 14 years experience	63,580	10	65,394	40	57,755	73	60,713	123
5 to 9 years experience	58,862	12	61,027	51	52,808	68	56,562	131
Under 5 years experience	56,512	12	52,935	53	47,825	99	50,112	164
All Positions	**$73,363**	**947**	**$72,455**	**2,834**	**$68,335**	**4,731**	**$70,266**	**8,512**

Canadian salaries are expressed in US dollars. Tables 31–34 show Canadian salaries in Canadian dollars. Excludes medical and law libraries.

( ) Indicates the number of ARL libraries in each category.

‡ Salary data are not published when fewer than four individuals are involved.

TABLE 22: YEARS OF EXPERIENCE OF ARL UNIVERSITY LIBRARIANS BY POSITION AND TYPE OF INSTITUTION, FY 2009–2010

Position	CANADIAN (15) Years	No.	PRIVATE (31) Years	No.	PUBLIC (68) Years	No.	TOTAL (114) Years	No.
Director	32.0	15	32.9	31	33.3	68	33.0	114
Associate Director	23.3	40	26.2	96	25.8	180	25.6	316
Assistant Director	24.2	19	25.2	67	23.8	84	24.4	170
Head, Branch	22.0	60	22.3	132	22.0	295	22.0	487
Functional Specialist	14.4	180	14.0	781	13.2	1,148	13.6	2,109
Subject Specialist	14.7	123	17.2	396	16.3	614	16.4	1,133
Dept. Head:								
Acquisitions	21.1	15	20.9	28	19.7	69	20.2	112
Reference	18.9	15	21.2	41	20.1	52	20.3	108
Cataloging	24.0	11	21.8	56	21.6	82	21.8	149
Serials	24.0	4	24.3	11	17.4	15	20.8	30
Documents/Maps	25.3	8	17.2	14	20.5	37	20.4	59
Circulation	18.7	14	16.5	18	19.6	51	18.8	83
Rare Books/Manuscripts	23.9	8	21.1	30	23.6	52	22.8	90
Computer Systems	20.7	7	18.8	23	20.0	43	19.7	73
Other	18.3	67	20.4	201	20.2	386	20.1	654
Reference:								
Over 14 years experience	25.6	83	25.7	150	25.1	343	25.3	576
10 to 14 years experience	12.0	29	11.9	61	11.9	122	11.9	212
5 to 9 years experience	6.9	71	7.1	67	7.1	168	7.0	306
Under 5 years experience	2.3	61	2.6	48	2.6	145	2.5	254
Cataloging:								
Over 14 years experience	29.2	37	26.0	165	26.4	199	26.5	401
10 to 14 years experience	12.4	10	11.6	47	12.3	49	12.0	106
5 to 9 years experience	6.9	9	7.0	64	6.6	68	6.8	141
Under 5 years experience	2.0	10	2.4	48	2.6	54	2.5	112
Other:								
Over 14 years experience	25.3	17	23.4	115	25.6	167	24.7	299
10 to 14 years experience	12.1	10	11.7	40	11.8	73	11.8	123
5 to 9 years experience	7.5	12	6.9	51	7.1	68	7.1	131
Under 5 years experience	1.8	12	2.5	53	2.4	99	2.4	164
All Positions	**16.5**	**947**	**17.2**	**2,834**	**17.0**	**4,731**	**17.0**	**8,512**

Excludes medical and law libraries.
( ) Indicates the number of ARL libraries in each category.

TABLE 23: NUMBER AND AVERAGE SALARIES OF ARL UNIVERSITY LIBRARIANS BY POSITION AND SIZE OF PROFESSIONAL STAFF, FY 2009–2010

Position	STAFF OVER 110 (17)† Salary	No.	STAFF 75–110 (18) Salary	No.	STAFF 50–74 (47) Salary	No.	STAFF 26–49 (32)‡ Salary	No.
Director	$231,501	17	$210,533	18	$189,054	47	$182,482	32
Associate Director	134,748	70	119,139	77	109,188	108	109,691	61
Assistant Director	115,943	46	88,907	34	101,340	67	100,112	23
Head, Branch	84,603	167	82,727	78	76,016	163	73,782	79
Functional Specialist	65,859	785	66,668	408	59,080	651	59,548	265
Subject Specialist	69,550	380	68,675	209	62,060	451	58,252	93
Dept. Head:								
Acquisitions	75,996	23	84,002	16	70,314	48	71,917	25
Reference	85,296	31	74,170	8	74,368	41	77,612	28
Cataloging	80,354	50	74,170	19	68,369	52	73,610	28
Serials	73,900	12	71,703	5	78,001	6	69,779	7
Documents/Maps	70,362	15	71,369	9	69,968	20	64,888	15
Circulation	76,734	22	71,560	16	66,193	31	66,553	14
Rare Books/Manuscripts	95,586	13	87,079	17	77,219	34	79,794	26
Computer Systems	104,411	13	96,813	10	83,427	36	87,657	14
Other	81,749	187	78,049	125	74,009	256	76,960	86
Reference:								
Over 14 years experience	68,964	132	69,578	113	67,048	180	67,756	151
10 to 14 years experience	61,504	56	61,308	36	60,023	71	58,673	49
5 to 9 years experience	59,880	73	56,085	70	52,506	90	53,655	73
Under 5 years experience	51,246	44	50,882	48	46,687	104	48,136	58
Cataloging:								
Over 14 years experience	70,998	151	62,239	80	60,649	122	65,583	48
10 to 14 years experience	64,400	41	54,950	16	54,489	36	53,251	13
5 to 9 years experience	59,274	62	52,141	27	51,655	33	49,961	19
Under 5 years experience	54,235	45	47,118	17	46,203	40	45,378	10
Other:								
Over 14 years experience	71,771	93	73,263	66	65,847	91	58,806	49
10 to 14 years experience	64,406	40	62,684	37	59,384	27	50,988	19
5 to 9 years experience	61,041	49	55,350	32	54,324	35	49,739	15
Under 5 years experience	51,805	60	50,375	39	49,903	50	43,356	15
All Positions	**$72,800**	**2,677**	**$71,848**	**1,630**	**$67,681**	**2,890**	**$68,829**	**1,315**

Canadian salaries are expressed in US dollars. For average Canadian salaries (expressed in US dollars) refer to Table 21; Tables 31–34 show Canadian salaries in Canadian dollars.

Excludes medical and law libraries.

( ) Indicates the number of ARL libraries in each category.

† In 1995–1996 and earlier, the first column of this table reported staff over 124; in 1996–1998 over 120; in 1998–1999 over 115; and since 1999–2000, over 110.

‡ No ARL library has fewer than 26 professional staff members.

Table 24: Years of Experience of ARL University Librarians by Position and Size of Professional Staff, FY 2009–2010

Position	Staff Over 110 (17)† Years	No.	Staff 75–110 (18) Years	No.	Staff 50–74 (47) Years	No.	Staff 26-49 (32)‡ Years	No.
Director	34.7	17	32.1	18	32.4	47	33.4	32
Associate Director	26.4	70	25.9	77	24.6	108	26.1	61
Assistant Director	25.7	46	21.9	34	24.3	67	25.4	23
Head, Branch	22.4	167	21.6	78	21.9	163	22.0	79
Functional Specialist	13.3	785	14.1	408	13.6	651	14.0	265
Subject Specialist	16.1	380	17.3	209	16.8	451	14.1	93
Dept. Head:								
Acquisitions	20.8	23	24.3	16	19.2	48	18.7	25
Reference	21.8	31	18.5	8	20.2	41	19.4	28
Cataloging	22.7	50	22.3	19	21.9	52	20.0	28
Serials	23.8	12	17.0	5	21.7	6	17.6	7
Documents/Maps	21.3	15	19.0	9	20.8	20	19.9	15
Circulation	20.3	22	16.1	16	18.5	31	19.9	14
Rare Books/Manuscripts	24.8	13	22.2	17	22.4	34	22.8	26
Computer Systems	20.4	13	22.3	10	17.8	36	21.9	14
Other	22.1	187	18.6	125	18.9	256	21.5	86
Reference:								
Over 14 years experience	26.4	132	25.5	113	25.0	180	24.6	151
10 to 14 years experience	12.1	56	11.8	36	11.9	71	11.9	49
5 to 9 years experience	7.2	73	6.8	70	7.0	90	7.2	73
Under 5 years experience	2.4	44	2.8	48	2.3	104	2.8	58
Cataloging:								
Over 14 years experience	26.5	151	25.8	80	27.0	122	26.2	48
10 to 14 years experience	11.8	41	12.2	16	12.1	36	12.2	13
5 to 9 years experience	6.9	62	6.8	27	6.8	33	6.9	19
Under 5 years experience	2.6	45	2.1	17	2.6	40	2.2	10
Other:								
Over 14 years experience	25.5	93	24.9	66	25.0	91	22.7	49
10 to 14 years experience	12.0	40	11.8	37	11.8	27	11.3	19
5 to 9 years experience	7.0	49	7.3	32	6.9	35	7.3	15
Under 5 years experience	2.5	60	2.3	39	2.4	50	2.1	15
All Positions	**16.9**	**2,677**	**16.9**	**1,630**	**17.1**	**2,890**	**17.5**	**1,315**

Excludes medical and law libraries.

( ) Indicates the number of ARL libraries in each category.

† In 1995–1996 and earlier, the first column of this table reported staff over 124; in 1996–1998 over 120; in 1998–1999 over 115; and since 1999–2000, over 110.

‡ No ARL library has fewer than 26 professional staff members.

TABLE 25: AVERAGE SALARIES OF ARL UNIVERSITY LIBRARIANS BY POSITION AND GEOGRAPHIC REGION, FY 2009–2010

Position	Northeast — New England (9)	Northeast — Middle Atlantic (14)	North Central — East N. Central (17)	North Central — West N. Central (7)	South Atlantic (18)	South — East S. Central (6)	South — West S. Central (9)	West — Mountain (7)	West — Pacific (12)	Canada (15)	Total (114)
Director	$215,663	$234,070	$199,831	$188,846	$214,658	$173,289	$195,091	$173,289	$197,347	$151,500	$196,930
Associate Director	132,057	127,324	108,684	111,301	122,704	106,459	105,505	110,789	123,410	109,191	117,372
Assistant Director	108,684	112,387	96,868	104,472	104,992	87,790	92,931	108,429	103,344	91,609	102,639
Head, Branch	92,030	85,599	74,371	74,560	70,196	73,300	73,928	80,372	82,776	86,859	79,673
Functional Specialist	72,734	64,583	56,930	61,943	60,575	53,101	56,520	60,992	67,537	65,785	63,130
Subject Specialist	73,269	67,486	62,113	58,637	59,366	56,221	54,716	63,045	74,134	65,527	65,480
Dept. Head:											
Acquisitions	81,851	71,368	70,429	69,753	68,732	62,677	65,324	81,093	80,235	83,456	73,794
Reference	88,962	78,399	73,294	75,884	78,607	‡	69,091	78,678	84,306	72,514	78,331
Cataloging	87,877	73,301	70,314	67,227	67,473	61,251	72,508	78,015	82,062	80,090	74,299
Serials	‡	75,288	‡		73,738	‡	‡	‡	‡	78,717	73,392
Documents/Maps	‡	71,004	62,477	70,783	62,413	‡	64,425	62,861	‡	83,961	68,990
Circulation	82,265	70,590	68,712	55,867	72,759	‡	58,969	‡	84,618	69,888	70,082
Rare Books/Manuscripts	89,859	88,705	85,331	78,555	82,816	75,512	68,514	73,617	83,749	83,843	82,479
Computer Systems	100,835	84,289	84,358	‡	89,153	‡	89,869	88,936	95,481	82,756	89,809
Other	82,650	79,835	79,047	62,847	76,472	69,109	67,087	75,612	84,314	80,848	77,382
Reference:											
Over 14 years experience	73,778	66,724	66,678	58,267	63,645	61,156	51,501	62,709	72,949	80,653	68,169
10 to 14 years experience	65,423	57,944	57,473	54,933	56,347	55,175	51,250	57,463	60,155	70,692	60,320
5 to 9 years experience	65,190	54,391	52,755	52,907	50,592	50,553	47,287	52,010	53,934	61,424	55,358
Under 5 years experience	50,469	47,623	48,346	46,979	46,125	45,409	41,451	46,262	47,115	54,104	48,600
Cataloging:											
Over 14 years experience	73,125	65,081	59,332	58,902	59,632	57,514	55,583	61,526	73,704	73,160	65,454
10 to 14 years experience	65,754	54,555	55,520	53,786	53,148	48,866	54,964	‡	62,269	57,874	58,240
5 to 9 years experience	63,843	54,288	50,207	47,208	51,739	‡	49,093	47,931	52,763	63,124	54,870
Under 5 years experience	56,138	46,801	48,744	42,956	44,959	42,164	44,891	45,573	48,858	53,444	49,496
Other:											
Over 14 years experience	72,993	74,748	69,092	66,048	58,500	64,549	58,204	66,323	76,954	77,347	68,173
10 to 14 years experience	73,003	66,336	58,532	49,732	59,117	50,193	58,546	48,921	65,029	63,580	60,713
5 to 9 years experience	64,889	61,887	54,559	54,190	52,213	54,746	48,913	50,846	51,340	58,862	56,562
Under 5 years experience	57,683	50,975	47,795	47,224	48,089	40,383	44,551	48,955	48,582	56,512	50,112
All Positions:											
Average Salary	$76,371	$73,127	$66,434	$64,744	$67,850	$62,872	$62,938	$68,341	$75,283	$73,363	$70,266
No. of Staff	1,119	1,194	1,338	466	1,161	305	607	413	962	947	8,512

Canadian salaries are expressed in US dollars. Excludes medical and law libraries.
( ) Indicates number of ARL libraries included.
‡ Salary data are not published when fewer than four individuals are involved.

ARL UNIVERSITY LIBRARIES BY GEOGRAPHIC REGION

Region	No. of Libraries	ARL University Libraries Included	States/Provinces Included
Northeast			
1. New England	9	Boston University, Boston College, Brown, Connecticut, Dartmouth, Harvard, Massachusetts Institute of Technology, Massachusetts, Yale	Conn., Mass., Me., N.H., R.I., Vt.
2. Middle Atlantic	14	Columbia; Cornell; New York; Pennsylvania; Pennsylvania State; Pittsburgh; Princeton; Rochester; Rutgers; State University of New York: Albany, Buffalo, Stony Brook; Syracuse; Temple	N.J., N.Y., Pa.
North Central			
3. East North Central	17	Case Western Reserve, Chicago, Cincinnati, Illinois-Chicago, Illinois-Urbana, Indiana, Kent State, Michigan, Michigan State, Notre Dame, Northwestern, Ohio University, Ohio State, Purdue, Southern Illinois, Wayne State, Wisconsin	Ill., Ind., Mich., Ohio, Wis.
4. West North Central	7	Iowa, Iowa State, Kansas, Minnesota, Missouri, Nebraska, Washington U.-St. Louis	Iowa, Kan., Minn., Mo., Neb., N. Dak., S. Dak.
South			
5. South Atlantic	18	Delaware, Duke, Emory, Florida, Florida State, Georgia, Georgia Tech., Georgetown, George Washington, Howard, Johns Hopkins, Maryland, Miami, North Carolina, North Carolina State, South Carolina, Virginia, Virginia Tech	Del., DC, Fla., Ga., Md., N.C., S.C., Va., W. Va.
6. East South Central	6	Alabama, Auburn, Kentucky, Louisville, Tennessee, Vanderbilt	Ala., Ky., Miss., Tenn.
7. West South Central	9	Houston, Louisiana State, Oklahoma, Oklahoma State, Rice, Texas, Texas A&M, Texas Tech, Tulane	Ark., La., Okla., Tex.
West			
8. Mountain	7	Arizona, Arizona State, Brigham Young, Colorado, Colorado State, New Mexico, Utah	Ariz., Colo., Idaho, Mont., Nev., N. Mex., Utah, Wyo.
9. Pacific	12	University of California: Berkeley, Davis, Irvine, Los Angeles, Riverside, San Diego, Santa Barbara; Hawaii; Oregon; Southern California; Washington; Washington State	Alaska, Calif., Hawaii, Ore., Wash.
Canada	15	Alberta, British Columbia, Calgary, Guelph, Laval, McGill, McMaster, Manitoba, Montreal, Queen's, Saskatchewan, Toronto, Waterloo, Western Ontario, York	Alta., B.C., Man., N. Br., Newf., N.S., Ont., P.E.I., Que., Sask.

Regions are based on the classification used by the US Bureau of the Census in tabulations of the Current Population Survey.

US ARL University Libraries

Tables 26–30

TABLE 26: AVERAGE SALARIES OF US ARL UNIVERSITY LIBRARIANS BY POSITION AND YEARS OF EXPERIENCE, FY 2009–2010

Position	0–3 Years	4–7 Years	8–11 Years	12–15 Years	16–19 Years	20–23 Years	24–27 Years	28–31 Years	32–35 Years	over 35 Years
Director	.	.	‡	‡	.	$209,850	$206,337	$192,893	$210,036	$203,299
Associate Director	.	$85,860	$93,486	$110,157	$116,404	117,223	119,223	119,284	126,264	129,548
Assistant Director	‡	74,889	87,909	94,991	113,752	101,848	103,980	108,917	114,648	106,707
Head, Branch	$55,278	58,603	68,229	72,234	76,652	79,290	80,266	82,408	92,624	91,929
Functional Specialist	48,936	55,086	60,439	65,882	67,555	70,131	76,942	74,784	81,678	79,013
Subject Specialist	49,029	54,265	61,162	66,576	67,741	71,851	72,012	75,569	79,450	81,860
Dept. Head:										
Acquisitions	56,586	63,563	62,508	66,713	73,909	73,597	73,655	82,185	80,432	89,880
Reference	‡	63,395	74,350	77,044	81,253	75,965	83,329	91,015	84,982	92,183
Cataloging	49,023	60,128	60,371	70,565	72,223	75,540	79,896	76,220	91,878	77,783
Serials	.	‡	61,165	‡	84,875	74,340	‡	‡	‡	‡
Documents/Maps	52,291	57,222	58,099	64,369	62,681	‡	71,402	76,173	‡	77,586
Circulation	47,653	61,263	56,144	71,724	75,010	74,109	71,206	96,695	79,885	83,665
Rare Books/Manuscripts	‡	.	71,046	73,313	79,376	74,000	90,934	84,751	95,998	93,351
Computer Systems	78,463	‡	90,190	89,679	91,472	84,314	92,391	99,212	103,334	.
Other	52,942	60,972	66,554	74,860	80,315	79,575	80,071	81,708	87,534	88,391
Public Services	47,769	51,510	55,269	57,325	62,277	58,769	63,425	67,742	64,886	69,142
Technical Services	48,153	53,934	57,872	55,793	60,776	63,866	61,788	63,732	77,344	75,299
Administrative Services	53,143	52,991	68,453	64,676	71,233	70,245	91,779	75,829	81,819	92,079
Reference	46,204	50,592	56,496	59,787	60,235	65,383	67,122	69,138	71,565	71,620
Cataloger	48,580	52,915	57,190	58,414	61,900	64,470	64,059	65,934	66,148	68,588
All Positions:										
Average Salary	$48,975	$54,505	$61,403	$67,101	$71,331	$74,909	$80,071	$84,387	$93,192	$93,943
Number of Staff	837	975	1,101	865	767	746	651	622	524	477

Excludes Canadian libraries.

Excludes medical and law libraries.

‡ Salary data are not published when fewer than four individuals are involved.

. No positions reported in this category.

TABLE 27: NUMBER AND AVERAGE SALARIES OF MINORITY US ARL UNIVERSITY LIBRARIANS BY POSITION AND SEX, FY 2009–2010

Position	WOMEN Salary	No.	MEN Salary	No.	TOTAL Salary	No.
Director	‡	4	‡	3	$174,493	7
Associate Director	‡	17	‡	3	117,635	20
Assistant Director	‡	3	‡	6	106,970	9
Head, Branch	70,496	32	88,641	14	76,019	46
Functional Specialist	59,836	142	63,696	123	61,628	265
Subject Specialist	63,406	140	65,048	60	63,898	200
Dept. Head:						
Acquisitions	‡	7	‡	2	75,881	9
Reference	75,228	5	.		75,228	5
Cataloging	‡	13	‡	1	72,247	14
Serials	‡	2	.		‡	2
Documents/Maps	‡	2	‡	1	‡	3
Circulation	‡	5	‡	3	73,467	8
Rare Books/Manuscripts	‡	5	‡	2	75,803	7
Computer Systems	‡	3	‡	8	82,953	11
Other	75,136	42	78,975	17	76,242	59
Reference:						
Over 14 years experience	69,371	44	67,086	17	68,734	61
10 to 14 years experience	61,337	13	59,038	7	60,532	20
5 to 9 years experience	53,947	29	57,244	7	54,588	36
Under 5 years experience	46,929	31	47,963	8	47,141	39
Cataloging:						
Over 14 years experience	62,158	40	71,254	12	64,257	52
10 to 14 years experience	59,078	14	61,525	6	59,812	20
5 to 9 years experience	52,110	22	55,600	10	53,201	32
Under 5 years experience	‡	21	‡	3	50,312	24
Other:						
Over 14 years experience	55,135	31	61,786	12	56,991	43
10 to 14 years experience	53,124	11	45,823	4	51,177	15
5 to 9 years experience	51,928	19	71,544	5	56,015	24
Under 5 years experience	45,929	22	50,295	4	46,601	26
All Positions	**$63,452**	**719**	**$67,786**	**338**	**$64,838**	**1,057**

Excludes Canadian libraries.
Excludes medical and law libraries.
‡ Salary data are not published when fewer than four individuals are involved in either category.
. No positions reported in this category.

TABLE 28: NUMBER AND AVERAGE YEARS OF EXPERIENCE OF MINORITY US ARL UNIVERSITY LIBRARIANS BY POSITION AND SEX, FY 2009–2010

Position	WOMEN Years	No.	MEN Years	No.	TOTAL Years	No.
Director	29.0	4	31.3	3	30.0	7
Associate Director	27.5	17	24.0	3	27.0	20
Assistant Director	18.0	3	16.2	6	16.8	9
Head, Branch	21.2	32	18.6	14	20.4	46
Functional Specialist	13.2	142	11.9	123	12.6	265
Subject Specialist	14.5	140	12.9	60	14.0	200
Dept. Head:						
Acquisitions	16.1	7	5.5	2	13.8	9
Reference	15.6	5	.		15.6	5
Cataloging	18.8	13	9.0	1	18.1	14
Serials	17.0	2	.		17.0	2
Documents/Maps	6.5	2	12.0	1	8.3	3
Circulation	15.6	5	26.3	3	19.6	8
Rare Books/Manuscripts	15.6	5	18.5	2	16.4	7
Computer Systems	18.0	3	13.1	8	14.5	11
Other	20.6	42	20.0	17	20.4	59
Public Services	9.8	42	12.5	15	10.5	57
Technical Services	15.6	26	15.0	1	15.6	27
Administrative Services	11.3	15	12.0	9	11.6	24
Reference	13.1	117	14.2	39	13.4	156
Cataloger	14.0	97	16.2	31	14.6	128
All Positions	**14.8**	**719**	**14.0**	**338**	**14.5**	**1,057**

Includes Canadian libraries. See Table 33 for comparable figures in Canadian libraries only.
Excludes medical and law libraries. See Tables 40 and 47 for comparable figures in medical and law libraries.
. No positions reported in this category.

TABLE 29: NUMBER AND AVERAGE SALARIES OF US ARL UNIVERSITY LIBRARIANS BY YEARS OF EXPERIENCE AND SEX, FY 2009–2010

| | WOMEN | | MEN | | TOTAL | | % OF |
Experience	Salary	No.	Salary	No.	Salary	No.	TOTAL
0 – 3 years	$48,193	532	$50,339	305	$48,975	837	11%
4 – 7 years	53,685	606	55,851	369	54,505	975	13%
8 – 11 years	60,117	658	63,315	443	61,403	1,101	15%
12 – 15 years	66,030	526	68,763	339	67,101	865	11%
16 – 19 years	69,772	477	73,896	290	71,331	767	10%
20 – 23 years	73,665	476	77,102	270	74,909	746	10%
24 – 27 years	78,812	433	82,572	218	80,071	651	9%
28 – 31 years	82,158	373	87,725	249	84,387	622	8%
32 – 35 years	91,022	325	96,735	199	93,192	524	7%
over 35 years	93,602	319	94,632	158	93,943	477	6%
All Positions	**$68,787**	**4,725**	**$71,695**	**2,840**	**$69,879**	**7,565**	**100%**

Excludes Canadian libraries.
Excludes medical and law libraries.

TABLE 30: NUMBER AND AVERAGE SALARIES OF MINORITY US ARL UNIVERSITY LIBRARIANS BY YEARS OF EXPERIENCE AND SEX, FY 2009–2010

| | WOMEN | | MEN | | TOTAL | | % OF |
Experience	Salary	No.	Salary	No.	Salary	No.	TOTAL
0 – 3 years	$49,086	108	$52,603	50	$50,199	158	15%
4 – 7 years	52,179	117	57,931	48	53,852	165	16%
8 – 11 years	59,063	97	66,489	74	62,277	171	16%
12 – 15 years	64,348	92	67,103	51	65,330	143	14%
16 – 19 years	67,679	82	75,925	31	69,941	113	11%
20 – 23 years	74,658	73	72,769	24	74,190	97	9%
24 – 27 years	64,148	52	77,502	15	67,138	67	6%
28 – 31 years	72,729	29	79,092	18	75,166	47	4%
32 – 35 years	92,311	38	82,115	10	90,186	48	5%
over 35 years	84,323	31	97,108	17	88,851	48	5%
All Positions	**$63,452**	**719**	**$67,786**	**338**	**$64,838**	**1,057**	**100%**

Excludes Canadian libraries.
Excludes medical and law libraries.

CANADIAN ARL UNIVERSITY LIBRARIES

TABLES 31–34

Table 31: Filled Positions; Average, Median, and Beginning Professional Salaries; and Average Years of Professional Experience in Canadian ARL University Libraries, FY 2009–2010

Institution	Filled Positions FY 2010	Average Salaries		Median Salaries		Beginning Salaries		Average Yrs. Exp. FY 2010
		FY 2009	FY 2010	FY 2009	FY 2010	FY 2009	FY 2010	
Alberta ‡	62	$90,161	$98,203	$96,402	$104,209	$50,632	$50,632	18
British Columbia ‡	94	80,717	85,196	81,585	81,675	53,557	55,335	15
Calgary‡*	57	N/A	94,823	N/A	89,543	N/A	58,000	18
Guelph ‡	50	78,100	80,634	72,654	78,054	57,820	59,699	18
Laval	62	69,203	72,293	70,607	72,888	48,094	49,547	14
McGill	65	73,887	74,432	67,912	67,475	50,000	50,000	17
McMaster ‡	48	79,572	71,878	79,654	72,928	45,223	46,817	17
Manitoba ‡	41	90,172	95,500	94,294	100,070	47,444	48,820	23
Montreal ‡	92	70,042	73,199	67,304	69,243	42,160	43,130	15
Queen's	35	88,997	93,924	90,735	97,348	50,000	51,600	20
Saskatchewan ‡	40	86,263	89,027	86,845	91,994	50,101	52,731	17
Toronto ‡	143	91,747	91,249	92,700	87,729	51,900	51,900	16
Waterloo ‡	36	78,214	81,938	79,102	81,972	49,586	51,804	18
Western Ontario ‡	68	68,857	68,921	64,517	65,014	47,380	47,380	13
York ‡	54	96,722	96,016	89,352	90,210	49,000	49,000	17

Salaries are expressed in Canadian dollars. Directors are included in figures for average years of experience and filled positions, but not in the average and median salary statistics.

Excludes Canadian medical and law libraries. See Tables 35 and 42 for statistics related to medical and law library salaries.

‡ See Footnotes.

* Calgary became a member in FY 2010.

TABLE 32: NUMBER AND AVERAGE SALARIES OF CANADIAN ARL UNIVERSITY LIBRARIANS BY POSITION AND SEX, FY 2009–2010

Position	WOMEN Salary	No.	MEN Salary	No.	TOTAL Salary	No.
Director	$180,043	8	$172,996	7	$176,755	15
Associate Director	126,322	29	130,219	11	127,393	40
Assistant Director	105,866	12	108,619	7	106,880	19
Head, Branch	100,868	48	103,218	12	101,338	60
Functional Specialist	75,398	85	77,961	95	76,751	180
Subject Specialist	74,508	84	80,634	39	76,450	123
Dept. Head:						
Acquisitions	95,750	10	100,604	5	97,368	15
Reference	‡	14	‡	1	84,603	15
Cataloging	‡	9	‡	2	93,441	11
Serials	91,840	4	.		91,840	4
Documents/Maps	‡	5	‡	3	97,957	8
Circulation	‡	12	‡	2	81,539	14
Rare Books/Manuscripts	‡	5	‡	3	97,819	8
Computer Systems	‡	2	‡	5	96,552	7
Other	95,442	46	91,880	21	94,325	67
Reference:						
Over 14 years experience	93,618	61	95,431	22	94,098	83
10 to 14 years experience	81,827	20	83,917	9	82,476	29
5 to 9 years experience	72,061	53	70,493	18	71,663	71
Under 5 years experience	62,270	50	67,000	11	63,123	61
Cataloging:						
Over 14 years experience	86,326	23	83,761	14	85,355	37
10 to 14 years experience	‡	8	‡	2	67,522	10
5 to 9 years experience	‡	7	‡	2	73,647	9
Under 5 years experience	‡	7	‡	3	62,353	10
Other:						
Over 14 years experience	95,576	10	82,618	7	90,241	17
10 to 14 years experience	‡	7	‡	3	74,179	10
5 to 9 years experience	‡	11	‡	1	68,674	12
Under 5 years experience	‡	9	‡	3	65,932	12
All Positions	**$85,052**	**639**	**$86,714**	**308**	**$85,593**	**947**

Salaries are expressed in Canadian dollars.
Excludes Canadian medical and law libraries. See Tables 39 and 46 for salaries in medical and law libraries.
† Salary data are not published when fewer than four individuals are involved in either category.
. No positions reported in this category.

TABLE 33: NUMBER AND AVERAGE YEARS OF EXPERIENCE
OF CANADIAN ARL UNIVERSITY LIBRARIANS
BY POSITION AND SEX, FY 2009–2010

Position	WOMEN		MEN		TOTAL	
	Years	No.	Years	No.	Years	No.
Director	33.5	8	30.3	7	32.0	15
Associate Director	23.4	29	22.8	11	23.3	40
Assistant Director	23.2	12	26.0	7	24.2	19
Head, Branch	21.7	48	22.9	12	22.0	60
Functional Specialist	14.3	85	14.6	95	14.4	180
Subject Specialist	14.4	84	15.4	39	14.7	123
Dept. Head:						
Acquisitions	21.0	10	21.4	5	21.1	15
Reference	18.0	14	31.0	1	18.9	15
Cataloging	23.9	9	24.5	2	24.0	11
Serials	24.0	4	.		24.0	4
Documents/Maps	29.6	5	18.0	3	25.3	8
Circulation	20.9	12	5.5	2	18.7	14
Rare Books/Manuscripts	22.0	5	27.0	3	23.9	8
Computer Systems	23.5	2	19.6	5	20.7	7
Other	19.5	46	15.6	21	18.3	67
Public Services	6.2	6	8.0	4	6.9	10
Technical Services	11.5	11	16.3	6	13.2	17
Administrations	15.1	20	17.3	4	15.4	24
Reference	12.2	184	14.3	60	12.7	244
Cataloger	18.3	45	22.0	21	19.5	66
All Positions	**16.3**	**639**	**16.8**	**308**	**16.5**	**947**

Excludes Canadian medical and law libraries. See Tables 40 and 47 for figures in medical and law libraries.
. No positions reported in this category.

Table 34: Number and Average Salaries of Canadian ARL University Librarians by Years of Experience and Sex, FY 2009–2010

Experience	WOMEN		MEN		TOTAL		% OF TOTAL
	Salary	No.	Salary	No.	Salary	No.	
0 – 3 years	$61,655	91	$65,177	34	$62,613	125	13%
4 – 7 years	70,118	95	68,908	40	69,760	135	14%
8 – 11 years	76,241	92	76,657	46	76,380	138	15%
12 – 15 years	84,503	57	79,728	30	82,856	87	9%
16 – 19 years	87,804	57	95,036	29	90,243	86	9%
20 – 23 years	93,690	67	95,595	42	94,424	109	12%
24 – 27 years	101,882	48	95,053	25	99,543	73	8%
28 – 31 years	103,930	42	103,164	28	103,624	70	7%
32 – 35 years	99,969	43	104,388	18	101,273	61	6%
over 35 years	115,100	47	118,901	16	116,065	63	7%
All Positions	**$85,052**	**639**	**$86,714**	**308**	**$85,593**	**947**	**100%**

Salaries are expressed in Canadian dollars

Excludes Canadian medical and law libraries. See Tables 41 and 48 for salaries in medical and law libraries.

Note: the "% of Total" Column in the *ARL Annual Salary Survey 2008-2009* listed women's salaries instead of the total percentages. This error has been corrected in this edition.

ARL University Medical Libraries

Tables 35–41

TABLE 35: FILLED POSITIONS; AVERAGE, MEDIAN, BEGINNING PROFESSIONAL SALARIES; AND AVERAGE YEARS OF PROFESSIONAL EXPERIENCE IN ARL UNIVERSITY MEDICAL LIBRARIES, FY 2009–2010

Institution	Filled Positions	Average Salary	Median Salary	Beginning Salary	Average Yrs. Exp.
Alabama	3	‡	‡	$35,000	11.7
Alberta	4	‡	‡	43,398	22.5
Arizona	16	$63,771	$58,706	48,605	21.1
Boston University	12	52,015	47,400	43,000	7.0
British Columbia	12	70,669	74,711	47,429	17.0
Calgary	12	62,817	58,773	49,713	9.7
California, Davis	7	71,152	64,560	46,164	24.6
California, Irvine	1	‡	‡	46,164	1.0
California, Los Angeles	14	75,171	81,228	46,164	17.1
California, San Diego	11	68,461	68,982	46,164	13.5
Case Western Reserve	7	59,101	62,249	35,000	26.9
Cincinnati	17	57,738	49,004	40,000	19.7
Columbia	10	68,409	70,625	51,500	16.2
Connecticut	15	76,497	75,152	55,347	16.7
Cornell	9	78,010	78,320	51,000	21.6
Dartmouth	8	62,580	60,415	45,500	19.8
Duke	20	59,342	55,479	48,000	19.0
Emory	11	62,389	54,232	42,000	22.2
Florida	13	57,427	54,558	42,000	14.8
Florida State	4	‡	‡	42,000	16.3
George Washington	14	64,439	64,820	48,000	15.2
Georgetown	11	59,370	61,000	44,000	12.7
Harvard	45	74,775	70,001	48,800	11.3
Hawaii	4	‡	‡	42,660	14.5
Howard	4	‡	‡	45,000	26.0
Illinois, Chicago	23	57,276	53,823	47,000	12.9
Iowa	10	58,987	54,540	41,000	17.0
Johns Hopkins	25	65,575	62,644	44,000	13.8
Kansas	8	52,333	49,257	38,000	15.9
Kentucky	13	57,770	57,641	41,000	24.9
Louisiana State	1	‡	‡	36,000	4.0
Louisville	9	57,367	55,943	37,000	23.6
McGill	10	61,398	55,059	42,856	13.8
McMaster	8	58,080	65,069	40,128	12.1
Manitoba	18	65,780	62,390	41,845	16.2
Miami	10	71,977	72,165	50,000	20.7
Michigan	16	56,695	54,500	42,000	14.5
Minnesota	15	61,070	62,213	42,000	14.9

TABLE 35: FILLED POSITIONS; AVERAGE, MEDIAN, BEGINNING PROFESSIONAL SALARIES; AND AVERAGE YEARS OF PROFESSIONAL EXPERIENCE IN ARL UNIVERSITY MEDICAL LIBRARIES, FY 2009–2010

Institution	Filled Positions	Average Salary	Median Salary	Beginning Salary	Average Yrs. Exp.
Missouri	9	52,566	50,017	40,000	20.8
Montreal	10	61,382	59,349	45,332	15.1
Nebraska	15	62,725	57,200	45,000	18.9
New Mexico	16	64,016	61,309	39,372	19.4
New York University	31	$65,581	$59,518	$50,000	12.0
North Carolina	32	67,842	64,002	45,000	19.2
Northwestern	17	61,237	61,427	41,000	15.9
Ohio State	8	62,531	62,262	50,000	17.6
Oklahoma	9	59,514	60,019	35,000	18.4
Oklahoma State	4	‡	‡	38,000	22.0
Pennsylvania	10	63,867	60,221	43,500	20.6
Pennsylvania State	6	63,734	61,680	42,436	17.2
Pittsburgh	25	58,890	56,522	40,000	15.1
Queen's	9	71,491	68,905	44,227	15.9
Rochester	25	55,936	51,703	38,168	20.0
Saskatchewan	7	62,431	59,982	45,197	9.3
South Carolina	8	50,976	47,470	34,000	14.6
Southern California	15	69,020	64,516	48,500	16.7
Southern Illinois	6	62,521	66,592	41,000	24.5
SUNY Buffalo	13	66,442	63,552	45,000	22.0
SUNY Stony Brook	19	66,198	66,191	45,000	14.7
Temple	10	55,900	56,000	42,800	20.0
Tennessee, Knoxville	4	‡	‡	40,000	13.0
Tennessee, Memphis	13	54,873	51,091	45,000	22.0
Texas Tech	22	49,585	45,389	37,000	21.0
Toronto	12	80,426	90,617	44,484	17.7
Tulane	6	53,240	48,000	40,000	19.3
Utah	12	63,047	59,271	38,000	20.5
Vanderbilt	26	58,088	60,765	40,500	12.7
Virginia	13	65,396	66,000	45,000	21.9
Washington	23	63,297	59,148	42,600	20.3
Washington U.-St. Louis	22	61,797	53,847	40,000	20.7
Wayne State	4	‡	‡	45,000	18.3
Wisconsin	16	58,988	56,669	40,526	12.8
Yale	21	75,715	73,985	50,500	17.0

Directors are included in figures for filled positions and average years of experience, but not in either the average or median salary statistics.
Canadian salaries are expressed in US dollars.
‡ Salary data are not published when fewer than four individuals are involved.

TABLE 36: BEGINNING PROFESSIONAL SALARIES IN ARL UNIVERSITY MEDICAL LIBRARIES RANK ORDER TABLE, FY 2009–2010

Rank	Institution	Salary	Rank	Institution	Salary
1	Connecticut	55,347	38	McGill	42,856
2	Columbia	51,500	39	Temple	42,800
3	Cornell	51,000	40	Hawaii	42,660
4	Yale	50,500	41	Washington	42,600
5	Miami	50,000	42	Pennsylvania State	42,436
5	New York	50,000	43	Emory	42,000
5	Ohio State	50,000	43	Florida	42,000
8	Calgary	49,713	43	Florida State	42,000
9	Harvard	48,800	43	Michigan	42,000
10	Arizona	48,605	43	Minnesota	42,000
11	Southern California	48,500	48	Manitoba	41,845
12	Duke	48,000	49	Iowa	41,000
12	George Washington	48,000	49	Kentucky	41,000
14	British Columbia	47,429	49	Northwestern	41,000
15	Illinois, Chicago	47,000	49	Southern Illinois	41,000
16	Calif. Davis	46,164	53	Wisconsin	40,526
16	Calif. Irvine	46,164	54	Vanderbilt	40,500
16	Calif. Los Angeles	46,164	55	McMaster	40,128
16	Calif. San Diego	46,164	56	Cincinnati	40,000
20	Dartmouth	45,500	56	Missouri	40,000
21	Montreal	45,332	56	Pittsburgh	40,000
22	Saskatchewan	45,197	56	Tennessee, Knoxville	40,000
23	Howard	45,000	56	Tulane	40,000
23	Nebraska	45,000	56	Washington-St. Louis	40,000
23	North Carolina	45,000	62	New Mexico	39,372
23	SUNY Buffalo	45,000	63	Rochester	38,168
23	SUNY Stony Brook	45,000	64	Kansas	38,000
23	Tennessee, Memphis	45,000	64	Oklahoma State	38,000
23	Virginia	45,000	64	Utah	38,000
23	Wayne State	45,000	67	Louisville	37,000
31	Toronto	44,484	67	Texas Tech	37,000
32	Queen's	44,227	69	Louisiana State	36,000
33	Georgetown	44,000	70	Alabama	35,000
33	Johns Hopkins	44,000	70	Case Western Reserve	35,000
35	Pennsylvania	43,500	70	Oklahoma	35,000
36	Alberta	43,398	73	South Carolina	34,000
37	Boston University	43,000			

Beginning salary figures represent officially designated base, not necessarily salaries of actual incumbents.
Canadian salaries are expressed in US dollars.

TABLE 37: MEDIAN PROFESSIONAL SALARIES IN ARL UNIVERSITY MEDICAL LIBRARIES
RANK ORDER TABLE, FY 2009–2010

Rank	Institution	Salary	Rank	Institution	Salary
1	Toronto	90,617	38	Washington	59,148
2	California, Los Angeles	81,228	39	Calgary	58,773
3	Cornell	78,320	40	Arizona	58,706
4	Connecticut	75,152	41	Kentucky	57,641
5	British Columbia	74,711	42	Nebraska	57,200
6	Yale	73,985	43	Wisconsin	56,669
7	Miami	72,165	44	Pittsburgh	56,522
8	Columbia	70,625	45	Temple	56,000
9	Harvard	70,001	46	Louisville	55,943
10	California, San Diego	68,982	47	Duke	55,479
11	Queen`s	68,905	48	McGill	55,059
12	Southern Illinois	66,592	49	Florida	54,558
13	SUNY Stony Brook	66,191	50	Iowa	54,540
14	Virginia	66,000	51	Michigan	54,500
15	McMaster	65,069	52	Emory	54,232
16	George Washington	64,820	53	Washington U.-St. Louis	53,847
17	California, Davis	64,560	54	Illinois, Chicago	53,823
18	Southern California	64,516	55	Rochester	51,703
19	North Carolina	64,002	56	Tennessee, Memphis	51,091
20	SUNY Buffalo	63,552	57	Missouri	50,017
21	Johns Hopkins	62,644	58	Kansas	49,257
22	Manitoba	62,390	59	Cincinnati	49,004
23	Ohio State	62,262	60	Tulane	48,000
24	Case Western Reserve	62,249	61	South Carolina	47,470
25	Minnesota	62,213	62	Boston University	47,400
26	Pennsylvania State	61,680	63	Texas Tech	45,389
27	Northwestern	61,427		Alabama	*
28	New Mexico	61,309		Alberta	*
29	Georgetown	61,000		California, Irvine	*
30	Vanderbilt	60,765		Florida State	*
31	Dartmouth	60,415		Hawaii	*
32	Pennsylvania	60,221		Howard	*
33	Oklahoma	60,019		Louisiana State	*
34	Saskatchewan	59,982		Oklahoma State	*
35	New York University	59,518		Tennessee, Knoxville	*
36	Montreal	59,349		Wayne State	*
37	Utah	59,271			

Salaries of directors are not included in the calculation of medians. Alabama, Alberta, California-Irvine, Florida State, Hawaii, Howard, Louisiana State, Oklahoma State, Tennessee-Knoxville, and Wayne State are not ranked because they reported fewer than four individuals. Canadian salaries are expressed in US dollars.

TABLE 38: AVERAGE PROFESSIONAL SALARIES IN ARL UNIVERSITY MEDICAL LIBRARIES RANK ORDER TABLE, FY 2009–2010

Rank	Institution	Salary	Rank	Institution	Salary
1	Toronto	80,426	38	Northwestern	61,237
2	Cornell	78,010	39	Minnesota	61,070
3	Connecticut	76,497	40	Oklahoma	59,514
4	Yale	75,715	41	Georgetown	59,370
5	California, Los Angeles	75,171	42	Duke	59,342
6	Harvard	74,775	43	Case Western Reserve	59,101
7	Miami	71,977	44	Wisconsin	58,988
8	Queen`s	71,491	45	Iowa	58,987
9	California, Davis	71,152	46	Pittsburgh	58,890
10	British Columbia	70,669	47	Vanderbilt	58,088
11	Southern California	69,020	48	McMaster	58,080
12	California, San Diego	68,461	49	Kentucky	57,770
13	Columbia	68,409	50	Cincinnati	57,738
14	North Carolina	67,842	51	Florida	57,427
15	SUNY Buffalo	66,442	52	Louisville	57,367
16	SUNY Stony Brook	66,198	53	Illinois, Chicago	57,276
17	Manitoba	65,780	54	Michigan	56,695
18	New York University	65,581	55	Rochester	55,936
19	Johns Hopkins	65,575	56	Temple	55,900
20	Virginia	65,396	57	Tennessee, Memphis	54,873
21	George Washington	64,439	58	Tulane	53,240
22	New Mexico	64,016	59	Missouri	52,566
23	Pennsylvania	63,867	60	Kansas	52,333
24	Arizona	63,771	61	Boston University	52,015
25	Pennsylvania State	63,734	62	South Carolina	50,976
26	Washington	63,297	63	Texas Tech	49,585
27	Utah	63,047		Alabama	*
28	Calgary	62,817		Alberta	*
29	Nebraska	62,725		California, Irvine	*
30	Dartmouth	62,580		Florida State	*
31	Ohio State	62,531		Hawaii	*
32	Southern Illinois	62,521		Howard	*
33	Saskatchewan	62,431		Louisiana State	*
34	Emory	62,389		Oklahoma State	*
35	Washington U.-St. Louis	61,797		Tennessee, Knoxville	*
36	McGill	61,398		Wayne State	*
37	Montreal	61,382			

Salaries of directors are not included in the calculation of medians. Alabama, Alberta, California-Irvine, Florida State, Hawaii, Howard, Louisiana State, Oklahoma State, Tennessee-Knoxville, and Wayne State are not ranked because they reported fewer than four individuals. Canadian salaries are expressed in US dollars.

TABLE 39: NUMBER AND AVERAGE SALARIES OF ARL UNIVERSITY MEDICAL LIBRARIANS BY POSITION AND SEX, FY 2009–2010

Position	WOMEN Salary	No.	MEN Salary	No.	TOTAL Salary	No.
Head, Medical	$121,618	49	$129,622	19	$123,855	68
Associate Director	85,716	33	94,463	11	87,903	44
Assistant Director	67,564	33	64,503	7	67,028	40
Head, Branch	63,688	26	.		63,688	26
Functional Specialist	60,366	73	62,517	91	61,559	164
Subject Specialist	60,258	65	59,940	10	60,215	75
Dept. Head:						
Acquisitions	67,709	16	64,299	4	67,027	20
Reference	67,878	17	78,374	7	70,940	24
Cataloging	‡	10	‡	1	65,279	11
Serials	‡	6	‡	2	54,269	8
Documents/Maps	‡	1	.		‡	1
Circulation	59,032	11	62,983	8	60,696	19
Rare Books/Manuscripts	‡	2	‡	6	70,824	8
Computer Systems	78,337	5	87,697	9	84,354	14
Other	66,866	50	72,008	16	68,112	66
Reference:						
Over 14 years experience	64,369	94	65,642	18	64,574	112
10 to 14 years experience	61,674	27	65,117	8	62,461	35
5 to 9 years experience	55,685	41	58,381	13	56,334	54
Under 5 years experience	48,240	41	46,875	6	48,066	47
Cataloging:						
Over 14 years experience	‡	6	‡	2	62,813	8
10 to 14 years experience	‡	2	.		‡	2
5 to 9 years experience	50,278	5	.		50,278	5
Under 5 years experience	‡	2	.		‡	2
Other:						
Over 14 years experience	62,322	32	62,444	10	62,351	42
10 to 14 years experience	‡	11	‡	3	58,211	14
5 to 9 years experience	‡	16	‡	3	55,301	19
Under 5 years experience	45,239	12	44,788	8	45,059	20
All Positions	**$66,583**	**686**	**$69,796**	**262**	**$67,471**	**948**

Canadian salaries are expressed in US dollars.
‡ Salary data are not published when fewer than four individuals are involved in either category.
. No positions reported in this category.

TABLE 40: NUMBER AND AVERAGE YEARS OF EXPERIENCE OF ARL UNIVERSITY MEDICAL LIBRARIANS BY POSITION AND SEX, FY 2009–2010

Position	WOMEN		MEN		TOTAL	
	Years	No.	Years	No.	Years	No.
Head, Medical	29.8	49	29.1	19	29.6	68
Associate Director	25.7	33	25.4	11	25.6	44
Assistant Director	20.3	33	13.0	7	19.0	40
Head, Branch	18.3	26	.		18.3	26
Functional Specialist	14.2	73	11.5	91	12.7	164
Subject Specialist	15.8	65	12.7	10	15.4	75
Dept. Head:						
Acquisitions	20.4	16	15.3	4	19.4	20
Reference	21.2	17	22.6	7	21.6	24
Cataloging	19.5	10	33.0	1	20.7	11
Serials	16.2	6	14.5	2	15.8	8
Documents/Maps	19.0	1	.		19.0	1
Circulation	20.5	11	8.6	8	15.5	19
Rare Books/Manuscripts	29.0	2	24.2	6	25.4	8
Computer Systems	16.0	5	18.6	9	17.6	14
Other	18.5	50	13.8	16	17.3	66
Public Services	14.8	44	11.3	16	13.8	60
Technical Services	16.7	15	19.3	4	17.3	19
Administrative Services	16.3	12	14.3	4	15.8	16
Reference	15.0	203	14.1	45	14.8	248
Cataloger	12.4	15	26.0	2	14.0	17
All Positions	**17.7**	**686**	**15.2**	**262**	**17.0**	**948**

. No positions reported in this category.

TABLE 41: NUMBER AND AVERAGE SALARIES OF ARL UNIVERSITY MEDICAL LIBRARIANS BY YEARS OF EXPERIENCE AND SEX, FY 2009–2010

Experience	WOMEN Salary	No.	MEN Salary	No.	TOTAL Salary	No.	% OF TOTAL
0 – 3 years	$49,526	72	$51,643	39	$50,270	111	12%
4 – 7 years	53,948	86	55,351	34	54,345	120	13%
8 – 11 years	59,471	103	66,052	45	61,472	148	16%
12 – 15 years	67,416	66	67,047	39	67,279	105	11%
16 – 19 years	64,403	68	77,676	19	67,301	87	9%
20 – 23 years	66,349	52	82,710	21	71,056	73	8%
24 – 27 years	72,372	69	77,918	18	73,520	87	9%
28 – 31 years	75,216	75	82,278	22	76,818	97	10%
32 – 35 years	87,271	54	94,280	17	88,949	71	7%
over 35 years	90,704	41	96,915	8	91,718	49	5%
All Positions	**$66,583**	**686**	**$69,796**	**262**	**$67,471**	**948**	**100%**

Canadian salaries are expressed in US dollars.

ARL University Law Libraries

Tables 42–48

TABLE 42: FILLED POSITIONS; AVERAGE, MEDIAN, BEGINNING PROFESSIONAL SALARIES; AND AVERAGE YEARS OF EXPERIENCE IN ARL UNIVERSITY LAW LIBRARIES, FY 2009–2010

Institution	Filled Positions	Average Salary	Median Salary	Beginning Salary	Average Yrs. Exp.
Alabama	10	$59,066	$57,320	$52,000	19.3
Alberta	4	‡	‡	45,594	28.5
Arizona	10	63,849	65,000	50,000	14.8
Arizona State	7	65,701	66,584	45,000	21.6
Boston University	11	70,830	64,300	55,000	16.8
Boston College	14	74,773	77,625	50,000	19.1
British Columbia	3	‡	‡	47,429	23.3
Calgary	3	‡	‡	49,713	18.0
California, Davis	8	73,380	68,892	46,164	17.9
California, Irvine	1	‡	‡	46,164	9.0
California, Los Angeles	15	78,860	84,455	46,164	14.1
Case Western Reserve	12	67,090	66,149	35,000	19.3
Cincinnati	6	64,155	53,580	44,000	22.2
Colorado	8	72,313	59,901	45,000	17.9
Columbia	18	71,168	61,116	51,500	11.7
Connecticut	11	75,922	74,684	41,857	18.6
Cornell	7	79,220	73,015	58,000	15.6
Duke	11	74,075	68,575	55,000	17.8
Emory	9	58,084	52,941	44,000	12.9
Florida	9	61,129	57,699	50,000	17.2
Florida State	10	55,938	53,494	52,000	20.0
George Washington	22	85,686	80,007	58,000	13.9
Georgetown	25	74,865	70,000	50,000	11.5
Georgia	8	60,001	56,901	40,000	17.0
Harvard	39	73,096	68,525	48,800	14.6
Hawaii	5	84,551	81,193	55,000	15.6
Houston	12	54,915	51,500	51,000	16.0
Howard	6	48,423	49,914	45,000	20.7
Illinois, Urbana	10	61,284	59,129	54,000	15.5
Indiana	10	69,325	64,923	40,400	21.0
Iowa	17	76,488	70,750	41,000	21.3
Kansas	8	49,563	45,297	38,000	9.6
Kentucky	7	52,015	47,838	41,000	11.6
Louisiana State	9	57,380	55,846	40,000	17.2
Louisville	6	59,853	59,931	37,000	19.3
McGill	4	‡	‡	42,856	16.5
Manitoba	3	‡	‡	41,851	28.3
Miami	14	56,251	53,000	45,000	15.7
Michigan	12	78,454	70,553	48,000	15.8
Minnesota	14	75,686	68,200	46,000	20.0

Table 42: Filled Positions; Average, Median, Beginning Professional Salaries; and Average Years of Experience in ARL University Law Libraries, FY 2009–2010

Institution	Filled Positions	Average Salary	Median Salary	Beginning Salary	Average Yrs. Exp.
Missouri	8	54,645	57,327	40,000	13.6
Montreal	5	60,353	55,200	45,332	10.8
Nebraska	5	63,975	63,772	45,000	17.4
New Mexico	7	63,420	56,928	50,000	9.3
New York University	19	79,659	79,673	60,000	21.6
North Carolina	12	74,947	68,000	45,000	15.8
Northwestern	11	63,154	59,572	44,000	19.5
Notre Dame	13	71,539	66,248	41,200	18.4
Ohio State	7	68,558	63,173	42,000	13.6
Oklahoma	7	57,410	51,269	42,000	14.7
Oregon	6	56,465	57,846	42,000	20.8
Pennsylvania	15	70,502	63,865	43,500	17.3
Pennsylvania State	10	75,080	69,360	55,000	20.3
Queen`s	3	‡	‡	44,227	9.7
Rutgers, Camden	8	84,946	87,500	60,000	22.0
Rutgers, Newark	10	72,346	64,000	52,000	16.5
Saskatchewan	3	‡	‡	45,197	22.0
South Carolina	8	63,808	67,619	50,000	9.3
Southern Illinois	4	‡	‡	50,000	8.5
SUNY Buffalo	10	69,905	77,137	45,000	17.9
Syracuse	9	57,805	54,353	47,000	15.0
Temple	10	61,988	51,654	42,448	23.1
Tennessee	8	70,669	59,440	50,000	18.0
Texas	15	58,876	53,857	38,000	16.3
Texas Tech	8	63,439	65,549	47,000	13.3
Toronto	6	74,123	73,979	44,484	17.8
Tulane	7	58,420	56,970	40,000	17.6
Utah	8	57,095	52,530	41,500	16.5
Vanderbilt	5	68,154	59,830	40,500	20.0
Virginia	14	68,146	63,500	63,500	15.5
Washington	16	72,614	70,020	59,000	22.1
Washington U.-St. Louis	10	62,335	57,500	50,000	18.5
Wayne State	3	‡	‡	45,000	19.3
Western Ontario	3	‡	‡	40,610	14.3
Wisconsin	12	62,919	58,954	40,526	23.1
Yale	19	81,322	81,500	50,500	18.7
York	5	71,436	72,376	41,999	15.2

Directors are included in figures for filled positions and average years of experience, but not in either the average or median salary statistics.

Canadian salaries are expressed in US dollars.

‡ Salary data are not published when fewer than four individuals are involved.

TABLE 43: BEGINNING PROFESSIONAL SALARIES IN ARL UNIVERSITY LAW LIBRARIES
RANK ORDER TABLE, FY 2009–2010

Rank	Institution	Salary	Rank	Institution	Salary
1	Virginia	63,500	40	Arizona State	45,000
2	New York	60,000	40	Colorado	45,000
2	Rutgers, Camden Law	60,000	40	Howard	45,000
4	Washington	59,000	40	Miami	45,000
5	Cornell	58,000	40	Nebraska	45,000
5	George Washington	58,000	40	North Carolina	45,000
7	Boston University	55,000	40	SUNY Buffalo	45,000
7	Duke	55,000	40	Wayne State	45,000
7	Hawaii	55,000	48	Toronto	44,484
7	Pennsylvania State	55,000	49	Queen's	44,227
11	Illinois, Urbana	54,000	50	Cincinnati	44,000
12	Alabama	52,000	50	Emory	44,000
12	Florida State	52,000	50	Northwestern	44,000
12	Rutgers, Newark Law	52,000	53	Pennsylvania	43,500
15	Columbia	51,500	54	McGill	42,856
16	Houston	51,000	55	Temple	42,448
17	Yale	50,500	56	Ohio State	42,000
18	Arizona	50,000	56	Oklahoma	42,000
18	Boston College	50,000	56	Oregon	42,000
18	Florida	50,000	59	York	41,999
18	Georgetown	50,000	60	Connecticut	41,857
18	New Mexico	50,000	61	Manitoba	41,851
18	South Carolina	50,000	62	Utah	41,500
18	Southern Illinois	50,000	63	Notre Dame	41,200
18	Tennessee	50,000	64	Iowa	41,000
18	Washington-St. Louis	50,000	64	Kentucky	41,000
27	Calgary	49,713	66	Western Ontario	40,610
28	Harvard	48,800	67	Wisconsin	40,526
29	Michigan	48,000	68	Vanderbilt	40,500
30	British Columbia	47,429	69	Indiana	40,400
31	Syracuse	47,000	70	Georgia	40,000
31	Texas Tech	47,000	70	Louisiana State	40,000
33	Calif. Davis	46,164	70	Missouri	40,000
33	Calif. Irvine	46,164	70	Tulane	40,000
33	Calif. Los Angeles	46,164	74	Kansas	38,000
36	Minnesota	46,000	74	Texas	38,000
37	Alberta	45,594	76	Louisville	37,000
38	Montreal	45,332	77	Case Western Reserve	35,000
39	Saskatchewan	45,197			

Beginning salary figures represent officially designated base, not necessarily salaries of actual incumbents.
Canadian salaries are expressed in US dollars.

TABLE 44: MEDIAN PROFESSIONAL SALARIES IN ARL UNIVERSITY LAW LIBRARIES RANK ORDER TABLE, FY 2009–2010

Rank	Institution	Salary	Rank	Institution	Salary
1	Rutgers, Camden	87,500	39	Vanderbilt	59,830
2	California, Los Angeles	84,455	40	Northwestern	59,572
3	Yale	81,500	41	Tennessee	59,440
4	Hawaii	81,193	42	Illinois, Urbana	59,129
5	George Washington	80,007	43	Wisconsin	58,954
6	New York University	79,673	44	Oregon	57,846
7	Boston College	77,625	45	Florida	57,699
8	SUNY Buffalo	77,137	46	Washington U.-St. Louis	57,500
9	Connecticut	74,684	47	Missouri	57,327
10	Toronto	73,979	48	Alabama	57,320
11	Cornell	73,015	49	Tulane	56,970
12	York	72,376	50	New Mexico	56,928
13	Iowa	70,750	51	Georgia	56,901
14	Michigan	70,553	52	Louisiana State	55,846
15	Washington	70,020	53	Montreal	55,200
16	Georgetown	70,000	54	Syracuse	54,353
17	Pennsylvania State	69,360	55	Texas	53,857
18	California, Davis	68,892	56	Cincinnati	53,580
19	Duke	68,575	57	Florida State	53,494
20	Harvard	68,525	58	Miami	53,000
21	Minnesota	68,200	59	Emory	52,941
22	North Carolina	68,000	60	Utah	52,530
23	South Carolina	67,619	61	Temple	51,654
24	Arizona State	66,584	62	Houston	51,500
25	Notre Dame	66,248	63	Oklahoma	51,269
26	Case Western Reserve	66,149	64	Howard	49,914
27	Texas Tech	65,549	65	Kentucky	47,838
28	Arizona	65,000	66	Kansas	45,297
29	Indiana	64,923		Alberta	*
30	Boston University	64,300		British Columbia	*
31	Rutgers, Newark	64,000		Calgary	*
32	Pennsylvania	63,865		McGill	*
33	Nebraska	63,772		Manitoba	*
34	Virginia	63,500		Queen`s	*
35	Ohio State	63,173		Saskatchewan	*
36	Columbia	61,116		Southern Illinois	*
37	Louisville	59,931		Wayne State	*
38	Colorado	59,901		Western Ontario	*

Salaries of directors are not included in the calculation of medians. Alberta, British Columbia, Calgary, McGill, Manitoba, Queen's, Saskatchewan, Southern Illinois, Wayne State, and Western Ontario are not ranked because they reported fewer than four individuals. Canadian salaries are expressed in US dollars.

Table 45: Average Professional Salaries in ARL University Law Libraries
Rank Order Table, FY 2009–2010

Rank	Institution	Salary	Rank	Institution	Salary
1	George Washington	85,686	39	South Carolina	63,808
2	Rutgers, Camden	84,946	40	Texas Tech	63,439
3	Hawaii	84,551	41	New Mexico	63,420
4	Yale	81,322	42	Northwestern	63,154
5	New York University	79,659	43	Wisconsin	62,919
6	Cornell	79,220	44	Washington U.-St. Louis	62,335
7	California, Los Angeles	78,860	45	Temple	61,988
8	Michigan	78,454	46	Illinois, Urbana	61,284
9	Iowa	76,488	47	Florida	61,129
10	Connecticut	75,922	48	Montreal	60,353
11	Minnesota	75,686	49	Georgia	60,001
12	Pennsylvania State	75,080	50	Louisville	59,853
13	North Carolina	74,947	51	Alabama	59,066
14	Georgetown	74,865	52	Texas	58,876
15	Boston College	74,773	53	Tulane	58,420
16	Toronto	74,123	54	Emory	58,084
17	Duke	74,075	55	Syracuse	57,805
18	California, Davis	73,380	56	Oklahoma	57,410
19	Harvard	73,096	57	Louisiana State	57,380
20	Washington	72,614	58	Utah	57,095
21	Rutgers, Newark	72,346	59	Oregon	56,465
22	Colorado	72,313	60	Miami	56,251
23	Notre Dame	71,539	61	Florida State	55,938
24	York	71,436	62	Houston	54,915
25	Columbia	71,168	63	Missouri	54,645
26	Boston University	70,830	64	Kentucky	52,015
27	Tennessee	70,669	65	Kansas	49,563
28	Pennsylvania	70,502	66	Howard	48,423
29	SUNY Buffalo	69,905		Alberta	*
30	Indiana	69,325		British Columbia	*
31	Ohio State	68,558		Calgary	*
32	Vanderbilt	68,154		McGill	*
33	Virginia	68,146		Manitoba	*
34	Case Western Reserve	67,090		Queen's	*
35	Arizona State	65,701		Saskatchewan	*
36	Cincinnati	64,155		Southern Illinois	*
37	Nebraska	63,975		Wayne State	*
38	Arizona	63,849		Western Ontario	*

Salaries of directors are not included in the calculation of medians. Alberta, British Columbia, Calgary, McGill, Manitoba, Queen's, Saskatchewan, Southern Illinois, Wayne State, and Western Ontario are not ranked because they reported fewer than four individuals. Canadian salaries are expressed in US dollars.

Table 46: Number and Average Salaries of ARL University Law Librarians by Position and Sex, FY 2009–2010

Position	Women Salary	Women No.	Men Salary	Men No.	Total Salary	Total No.
Head, Law	$151,028	39	$155,267	38	$153,120	77
Associate Director	93,011	34	93,519	24	93,221	58
Assistant Director	90,055	24	89,016	10	89,749	34
Functional Specialist	59,123	28	64,963	26	61,935	54
Subject Specialist	75,055	22	70,698	12	73,518	34
Dept. Head:						
Acquisitions	63,699	26	57,183	8	62,166	34
Reference	77,914	18	77,104	10	77,625	28
Cataloging	73,337	24	64,112	4	72,020	28
Serials	‡	5	‡	2	70,492	7
Documents/Maps	‡	7	‡	2	71,695	9
Circulation	61,620	24	58,514	5	61,084	29
Rare Books/Manuscripts	‡	3	‡	1	75,779	4
Computer Systems	‡	3	‡	5	77,600	8
Other	73,100	23	72,652	12	72,946	35
Reference:						
Over 14 years experience	73,879	48	73,085	21	73,637	69
10 to 14 years experience	62,097	13	58,388	8	60,684	21
5 to 9 years experience	60,304	31	62,430	19	61,112	50
Under 5 years experience	59,009	51	55,372	25	57,813	76
Cataloging:						
Over 14 years experience	62,094	20	69,828	5	63,641	25
10 to 14 years experience	‡	8	‡	1	55,997	9
5 to 9 years experience	57,120	10	.		57,120	10
Under 5 years experience	‡	4	‡	2	56,707	6
Other:						
Over 14 years experience	61,965	11	63,175	6	62,392	17
10 to 14 years experience	‡	6	‡	1	65,941	7
5 to 9 years experience	‡	3	‡	3	55,251	6
Under 5 years experience	‡	9	‡	3	48,479	12
All Positions	**$75,424**	**494**	**$82,097**	**253**	**$77,684**	**747**

Canadian salaries are expressed in US dollars.
‡ Salary data are not published when fewer than four individuals are involved in either category.
. No positions reported in this category.

TABLE 47: NUMBER AND AVERAGE YEARS OF EXPERIENCE OF ARL UNIVERSITY LAW LIBRARIANS BY POSITION AND SEX, FY 2009–2010

Position	WOMEN		MEN		TOTAL	
	Years	No.	Years	No.	Years	No.
Associate Director	25.6	34	19.4	24	23.0	58
Assistant Director	21.5	24	23.3	10	22.0	34
Head, Law	28.2	39	24.0	38	26.1	77
Functional Specialist	11.4	28	9.8	26	10.6	54
Subject Specialist	19.0	22	16.9	12	18.3	34
Dept. Head:						
Acquisitions	20.9	26	14.8	8	19.5	34
Reference	14.9	18	19.8	10	16.6	28
Cataloging	26.9	24	21.5	4	26.1	28
Serials	23.0	5	7.0	2	18.4	7
Documents/Maps	27.4	7	20.0	2	25.8	9
Circulation	15.9	24	13.2	5	15.4	29
Rare Books/Manuscripts	16.0	3	9.0	1	14.3	4
Computer Systems	21.7	3	19.0	5	20.0	8
Other	17.9	23	15.6	12	17.1	35
Public Services	15.4	9	15.0	8	15.2	17
Technical Services	10.8	14	14.0	2	11.2	16
Administrative Services	19.5	6	14.3	3	17.8	9
Reference	11.6	143	10.7	73	11.3	216
Cataloger	17.4	42	18.8	8	17.6	50
All Positions	**17.6**	**494**	**15.8**	**253**	**17.0**	**747**

TABLE 48: NUMBER AND AVERAGE SALARIES OF ARL UNIVERSITY LAW LIBRARIANS BY YEARS OF EXPERIENCE AND SEX, FY 2009–2010

Experience	WOMEN Salary	No.	MEN Salary	No.	TOTAL Salary	No.	% OF TOTAL
0 – 3 years	$56,458	70	$54,409	35	$55,775	105	14%
4 – 7 years	60,703	66	60,500	36	60,631	102	14%
8 – 11 years	68,700	44	70,355	37	69,456	81	11%
12 – 15 years	69,566	64	87,351	26	74,704	90	12%
16 – 19 years	72,751	42	80,604	22	75,451	64	9%
20 – 23 years	84,884	41	83,140	27	84,192	68	9%
24 – 27 years	81,625	38	104,873	21	89,900	59	8%
28 – 31 years	85,595	49	110,547	25	94,024	74	10%
32 – 35 years	99,619	44	108,617	21	102,526	65	9%
over 35 years	‡	36	‡	3	106,669	39	5%
All Positions	**$75,424**	**494**	**$82,097**	**253**	**$77,684**	**747**	**100%**

Canadian salaries are expressed in US dollars.

‡ Salary data are not published when fewer than four individuals are involved in either category.

UNIVERSITY LIBRARY QUESTIONNAIRE AND INSTRUCTIONS

ARL Annual Salary Survey 2009–2010
University Library Questionnaire
General and Data Input (Excel) Instructions

http://www.arl.org/stats/annualsurveys/salary/

General Overview

- **Use the newly available Web form for your data submission:**
  University Libraries: http://www.formspring.com/forms/?661042-c6BynijupA
  Fill in Part I on the Web and upload your file for Part II through the same interface.
  NOTE: You must complete the entire submission in a single session. The Web interface does **NOT** allow you to return and edit your information once it is submitted.

- **This survey is concerned with professional positions only.** Since the criteria for determining professional status vary among libraries, there is no attempt to define the term "professional." Each library should report the salaries of those staff members it considers professionals, irrespective of faculty status or membership in a collective bargaining unit, including, when appropriate, staff who are not librarians in the strict sense of the term, such as computer experts, systems analysts, budget officers, etc.

- **Report individual salaries for the Main, Law, and Medical library on the separate template using Microsoft Excel (see http://www.arl.org/stats/annualsurveys/salary/salform09.shtml).** A generic template is available. Add your institution's ARL Library Institution Code [LibID]. (See http://www.arl.org/stats/annualsurveys/surveycoord/instno_inam.shtml if you do not know your code.)

- **Use "Percent" to determine if an employee works full-time or part-time.** All full-time employees have Percent = 1.00, i.e., they work 100% of a full-time schedule. If Percent is less than 1.00, then the employee works that fraction of a full-time schedule. For example, a 65% time appointment would be entered as 0.65. Calculate the percent appointment by dividing the amount of time an employee works by the amount considered to be the norm for full-time employment at your institution. For example, if a full-time appointment at your institution is 12 months at 40 hours per week:
  - A 9-month part-time appointment has Percent = 9/12, or 0.75.
  - An appointment at 30 hours per week has Percent = 30/40, also 0.75.
  - An appointment at 30 hours and 9 months has Percent = 0.75 x 0.75 = 0.56.
  Enter Percent with two decimal points.

- **Report salaries for both full-time and part-time professional positions.** Salaries for part-time positions should **NOT** be converted to their full-time equivalents. Report the actual part-time salary paid and indicate the percent appointment for that employee in the appropriate column.

- **Include salaries for all professional positions, regardless of whether the salaries come from regular library budget funds <u>or from special funds such as research grants</u>.** Please include all professionals involved in the provision of library services, including **<u>contract-supported positions</u>**.

- **The salary figures should be straight gross salary figures. <u>Do not include fringe benefits</u>.**

- **Provide explanatory footnotes to the reported figures, when necessary, at the end of Part I.** Footnotes will be included in the published survey, where appropriate.

- **After all data have been entered, make a backup copy of the complete file for your institution's master file.** Your backup should include individual names/ID numbers. NOTE: The data submitted to ARL should NOT include individual names/ID numbers, so <u>ARL will NOT be able to supply a copy of your institution's complete file next year</u>.

- **Please return the questionnaire the ARL Statistics and Measurement Program by September 30, 2009. Be sure to keep a complete copy of your return, including the electronic version of the data for your files.**

INSTRUCTIONS

Part I: Summary Data (Microsoft Word Form)

1. Part I of this survey deals with general information for the current fiscal year, 2009–2010.

2. Include the Beginning Professional Salary for Law and Medical libraries if included in the survey.

3. The Beginning Professional Salary is the salary that **would** be paid to a **newly hired professional without experience**, not necessarily the lowest professional salary paid. In reporting the beginning salary, please use a figure that is actually used or likely to be used for entry-level librarians hired by your library, even if it is your practice rarely to hire entry-level professionals without experience.

4. Please report the **2009–2010** Beginning Professional Salary <u>to the best of your knowledge</u> as it exists on July 1, 2009. Do not delay returning your survey with the expectation that more information will be available later.

5. The 2009–2010 Average and Median Salary figures will be calculated by ARL from the individual data supplied.

6. Be sure to fill in the name of the reporting library and the name of the person who prepares the report.

Part II: Individual Data (Microsoft Excel Form)

1. Part II of this survey requests information on salary, sex, minority status, rank, and years of experience for all filled positions for fiscal year 2009–2010. The survey requests information for individuals; aggregate data for each institution will be generated by computer. Vacant positions should be excluded from your report.

2. Data for the Main, Law, and Medical libraries should be reported on separate Excel files.

3. **Obtain the Excel file.** These instructions assume that you have Microsoft Excel available for use. If not, or if you have trouble opening the files in Excel, please call the ARL Statistics and Measurement Program at (202) 296-2296 or e-mail stats@arl.org.

4. The template Excel file is available at: http://www.arl.org/stats/annualsurveys/salary/salform09.shtml. This is a generic, blank file that can hold data for Main, Law, or Medical libraries. The file's name is "sal09xxxx. xls"; open the file and save it to your own computer by choosing "Save As" under the File menu. When saving the file, utilize ARL as the prefix for main library reports, use 09 to designate the year (2009-2010), and change the "xxxx" in its name to your ARL institution code number, e.g., "ARL091150.xls." Note: use MED for medical libraries, e.g., "MED091150," and LAW to denote law libraries, e.g., "LAW091150."

    The file contains columns labeled as follows:
    Required: Name/ID#, LibID, Page, Line, Salary, Job, Sex, OEOcat, Yrsexp, Rank, Percent
    Optional: Hisp, NatAm, Asian, Black, HawPI, White

    In the LibID column, enter your ARL Library Institution Code. (See http://www.arl.org/stats/annualsurveys/surveycoord/instno_inam.shtml if you do not know your code.) If you leave this column blank we will fill it in for you when we receive the data.

    Columns labeled "Page," "Line," and "Percent" are already filled for you. The numbers in the "Page" and "Line" columns will be used to identify these positions in case of data errors; do not change them. Ten "pages" of 25 lines each have been provided; if this is not sufficient to list all positions at your institution, copy and paste lines 1-25 of the last page as needed.

Entering Data for Part II: Individual Data (Microsoft Excel Form)

1. The "Name/ID#" column is for your internal use, to enter and verify information for staff members by name. ARL does not require that you submit the information in this field to ARL. Please delete this column before sending the file to ARL. Upon receiving this file, ARL will delete any data in this column if you have not deleted them already.

2. The "LibID" will hold your institution's ARL number, for identification purposes. If you do not know your ARL number, you can find it on the Web under ARL Library Institution Codes. If you leave this column blank, it will be filled in by ARL staff.

3. "Salary" should be entered as it existed on July 1, 2009. Please do not hold up the reporting process for later salary adjustments. Include all filled positions and exclude all vacant positions. Report the actual salary paid. Do not adjust part-time salaries to their full-time equivalents; ARL will do this during the data analysis and verification stage. Do not include fringe benefits.

4. Each position can have only one "Job" code, to be taken from the following list:
    DIRLIB Director of Libraries (includes Dean of Libraries and equivalent titles)

ASCDIR	Associate Director	
ASTDIR	Assistant Director	
HDMED	Head, Medical Library (Human Medicine only)	
HDLAW	Head, Law Library	
HDBR	Head, Other Branch Library (including Veterinary Medicine)	
FSPEC	Functional Specialist	
	ARCH	Archivists/Curators
	BUSI	Budget/Fiscal/Business Manager/Facilities
	HUMRES	Human Resources/Training/Staff Development
	ITS	Information Technology Systems

ITW	Information Technology Web Development
ITP	Information Technology Programming/Application Development
MEDIA	Media/Multimedia Specialists (including graphics)
PRES	Preservation/Conservation
SSPEC	Subject Specialist
HDACQ	Head, Acquisitions Department
HDCAT	Head, Catalog Department/Unit
HDCIRC	Head, Circulation
HDCOMP	Head, Library and Computer Systems
HDDOC	Head, Documents Department
HDMAP	Head, Map Room/Department
HDRBM	Head, Rare Book/Manuscripts Department
HDREF	Head, Reference Department
HDSER	Head, Serials Department
HDOTH	Head, Other Department/Service/Agency
CAT	Catalogers, both general and specialized
REF	Reference librarians, both general and specialized
PUBS	Public Services, non-supervisory, except reference librarians
TECH	Technical Services, non-supervisory, except catalogers
ADMIN	Administrative and other units, non-supervisory position

The position categories used in this survey are intended to correspond roughly with the activities carried on in libraries, not with any particular pattern of staff organization or nomenclature. Please use these categories in the manner you feel best applies to your library. If any individual has responsibilities described by more than one of the above categories, choose the category that is most typical of his/her general duties.

Associate or Assistant Director, and Head, Other Branch. Use these codes for all persons at these levels regardless of the area of specialty. If an assistant or associate director is also head of a department, choose the category that most reflects the general duties of the person currently in the position.

Specialists. These are of two kinds: Subject Specialists primarily build collections, but may also offer specialized reference and bibliographic services; Functional Specialists are media specialists or experts in management fields such as personnel, fiscal matters, systems, preservation, etc. Specialists may not be, strictly speaking, professional librarians (i.e., have an MLS). The "specialist" category would generally not be used for someone with significant supervisory responsibilities, who should instead be listed as a department head or assistant director (see also note under Assistant Department Head, below).

Functional Specialist sub-codes. Starting with the 2004–2005 Salary Survey, the ARL Statistics and Measurement Committee adopted a proposal from the ACRL Personnel Administrators and Staff Development Officers Discussion Group to break down the Functional Specialist category. For each position which would have been labeled FSPEC prior to 2004-05, instead please use one of the eight sub-codes (ARCH, BUSI, HUMRES, ITS, ITW, ITP, MEDIA, PRES) to describe that position. If you cannot determine which sub-code to use, please use the FSPEC code.

Department Heads. Department Heads not specifically included in the above list should be included under the category "Head, Other Department/Service/Agency." Head, Catalog Department should be used either for the department that handles all cataloging, or for the head of a specialized cataloging unit (e.g., copy cataloging or foreign languages). List the head of library automation and computer systems, applications, programming, etc.

as HDCOMP unless that person is also an Associate or Assistant Director, in which case use the appropriate administrative code. If there is an intermediate level of management between an Associate or Assistant Director and the professionals who actually carry out the analysis, programming, etc., use HDCOMP to define that intermediate level. Professionals who carry out analysis, programming, etc., should be listed as functional specialists (FSPEC).

Head, Acquisitions Department. Use HDACQ for all of the following positions: (a) head of a department that is responsible for the selection of material (or management of selection activities carried out on a basis encompassing more than a single organizational unit), but not responsible for the placement of orders, payment of invoices, etc.; (b) head of a department responsible for the placement of orders, maintaining on-order files, payment of invoices, etc., but not responsible for selection decisions; (c) head of a department responsible for both the selection decisions (or coordination of selection activities) and for acquiring the material. Libraries that split these two functions between two departments should report more than one professional with the position HDACQ.

[*Special note concerning Assistant Department Heads.* Assistant Department Heads who are responsible for major units and spend the bulk of their time in supervision and revision of the work of others should also be listed as "Head, Other Department/Service/Agency." See additional subcodes below for Head, Cataloging, and Head, Other Department. However, Assistant Head positions responsible for small units or for supervision only in the absence of the head should be reported as non-supervisory or specialist positions as appropriate.]

Administrative. Please note that ADMIN is not only for Administrative Services and related positions, but also can be applied to Public Relations/Communications, Development/Fundraising, and all other administrative and/or professional positions which do not have a logical home elsewhere.

5. **Please indicate "Sex" with the letter M or F,** indicating male or female, respectively.

6. **"OEOCat" minority status code**, for US university libraries only, should be indicated with one of the following code numbers. (Leave blank if a Canadian library):

        1 = Black
        2 = Hispanic
        3 = Asian or Pacific Islander
        4 = American Indian or Native Alaskan
        5 = Caucasian/Other

7. **"YrsExp," or total years of professional experience.** For most professional staff members this will mean counting the years since the MLS degree was awarded. When counting, do not subtract interim periods when an individual was not engaged in professional library employment if these periods are short in relation to the overall professional career. Count an academic year contract period as a full year. Be sure to include professional experience in previous positions and in other institutions. The figure should be rounded off to the nearest whole number; for example, a position with 14.5 years of experience would appear as 15.

8. **Indicate "Rank" using the following system of codes:**

0   The library director. Some systems also use 0 for assistant and/or associate directors.
1   Lowest level in the rank structure, such as an entry-level position.
2–8   Successively higher levels; for example, 5 indicates a higher rank than 2.
9   Rank cannot be determined, or, the individual is outside the organization's rank structure.

Responses concerning rank should be limited to professional librarians, and other professionals who occupy the same ranks as librarians. Leave the rank column blank for professionals who do not occupy these ranks or if the column is not applicable. For example, if the Library Business Officer holds a rank typically used for university administrators but not for librarians, do not supply a rank code for that individual, even if you have included salary and other data.

If multiple ranking structures are used for librarians and these structures are substantially different and not equivalent, enter individual rank information only for that group which represents the largest fraction of "rank-and-file" librarians.

The maximum number of ranks reported here should not exceed the maximum number of rank-levels reported in Part I for individual data under Rank structure. When counting the total number of rank levels, include ranks that may be unoccupied at the present time due to circumstances like unusually high turnover, hiring freezes, etc.

9. **"Percent"** is used to determine if an employee works full-time or part-time. All full-time employees have Percent = 1.00, i.e., they work 100% of a full-time schedule. If Percent is less than 1.00, then the employee works that fraction of a full-time schedule. For example, a 65% time appointment would be entered as 0.65. Calculate the percent appointment by dividing the amount of time an employee works by the amount considered to be the norm for full-time employment at your institution. For example, if a full-time appointment at your institution is 12 months at 40 hours per week:
   o A 9-month part-time appointment has Percent = 9/12, or 0.75.
   o An appointment at 30 hours per week has Percent = 30/40, also 0.75.
   o An appointment at 30 hours and 9 months has Percent = 0.75 x 0.75 = 0.56.
Enter Percent with two decimal points.

Optional Questions: The US Office of Management and Budget has revised the Standards for the Classification of Federal Data on Race and Ethnicity and according to the new standard there will be five minimum categories for data on race (American Indian or Alaska Native, Asian, Black or African American, Native Hawaiian or Other Pacific Islander, and White) and one category for data on ethnicity ("Hispanic or Latino"). **Respondents will be able to report more than one race by choosing multiple responses to the race question.** The purpose of the revised classification is to reflect the increasing diversity of the US population that has resulted primarily from growth in immigration and in interracial marriages. The new standards were used by the Bureau of the Census in the 2000 decennial census.[1] In light of these developments, we are collecting the new classification on race and ethnicity in the *ARL Annual Salary Survey on an optional* basis.

Ethnicity should be indicated by coding 1 to indicate if the person is of Hispanic or Latino ethnicity, and coding 0 otherwise. The definition of Hispanic or Latino ethnicity is: A person of Cuban, Mexican, Puerto Rican, Cuban, South or Central American, or other Spanish culture or origin, regardless of race.

Race should be indicated for US university libraries only, by choosing one or more responses among the five racial categories provided here; 1=yes and 0=no. You can select multiple racial categories for a person. The definitions of the five racial categories, listed with their respective column names, are:

American Indian or Alaska Native (NatAm): A person having origins in any of the original peoples of North and South America (including Central America) who maintains tribal affiliation or community attachment.

---

1 http://www.census.gov/population/www/socdemo/race/racefactcb.html

Asian (Asian): A person having origins in any of the original peoples of the Far East, Southeast Asia, or the Indian subcontinent including, for example, Cambodia, China, India, Japan, Korea, Malaysia, Pakistan, the Philippine Islands, Thailand, and Vietnam.

Black or African American (Black): A person having origins in any of the black racial groups of Africa.

Native Hawaiian or Other Pacific Islander (HawPI): A person having origins in any of the original peoples of Hawaii, Guam, Samoa, or other Pacific Islands.

White (White): A person having origins in any of the original peoples of Europe, the Middle East, or North Africa.

Submitting the Data for Part I and Part II on the Web

ARL is using the online services of FormSpring to collect the data. As part of its privacy policy, FormSpring pledges not to sell any collected information to third parties. For the complete FormSpring privacy policy, visit http://www.formspring.com/privacy.html. ARL also accepts Part I and Part II of the salary survey by e-mail from those users who may be uncomfortable submitting the files in FormSpring:

- University Libraries: http://www.formspring.com/forms/?661042-c6BynijupA

Be sure to have the electronic copy of your completed salary survey Excel file handy as you will be submitting this file via the FormSpring Web form. In addition to the completed Excel file, be prepared to provide the following information as well:

- The name, title, e-mail and phone number of the person who prepared the Excel file. The name, title, e-mail and phone number of your institution's contact person for the salary survey (if different from the person who prepared the Excel file)

- Indicate whether you are submitting salary information for one or more of the following: Main, Law, or Medical library, and the beginning professional salary and rank structure for each.

  For professional salary list the salary that would be paid to a newly hired professional without experience (even if local practice discourages hiring entry-level professionals without experience). Please report the 2009–2010 beginning professional salary to the best of your knowledge as it existed on July 1, 2009.

  For rank structure, list the number of unique levels in your institution's rank structure. If you have no levels in your rank structure, use 1. The number reported here should be equal to the highest number in the "Rank" column of your Excel file (i.e., the number of levels reported in your Excel file should equal the number of levels reported here).

- The names of the libraries that are included and excluded in your figures for the 'general libraries' (these can be main campus libraries or branch campus libraries), as well as any other explanatory information, should be indicated in a footnote. In your footnotes, report any information that would clarify the figures submitted: the inclusion and exclusion of branch campus libraries, a reporting date that is sooner/later than July 1, 2009, etc. Please make an effort to word your footnotes in a manner consistent with notes appearing in the published report, so that ARL can interpret your footnotes correctly.

Please return the completed questionnaire to the

ARL Statistics and Measurement Program by **September 30, 2009.**
For assistance, contact Martha Kyrillidou (martha@arl.org) or Les Bland (les@arl.org) or
David Green (david@arl.org) or Gary Roebuck (gary@arl.org).
Tel. 202-296-2296 or fax 202-872-0884.

http://www.arl.org/stats/annualsurveys/salary/

ARL ANNUAL SALARY SURVEY 2009–2010

UNIVERSITY LIBRARY QUESTIONNAIRE

Note: This is a copy of the form that you will submit electronically at:
http://www.formspring.com/forms/?661042-c6BynijupA

Part I: Summary Data

Reporting Institution_____ Date Returned to ARL_____

Report Prepared by (name)_____

Title_____

Email address _____ Phone number_____

Contact person (if different) _____

Title_____

E-mail address _____ Phone number_____

*(**Note**: ARL will calculate the 2009-2010 median and average professional salaries for your library from the individual data you supply in Part II (Excel form) of this questionnaire.)*

		Main	Law	Medical
1.	**Beginning Professional Salary**			
	Beginning professional salary for 2009–2010	_____	_____	_____

*(**Note**: The Information shown below must be completed for all three branches (i.e. Main, Law and Health Science Libraries) in Part1 of the online form).*

2. **Rank Structure**.

Indicate the number of levels in your institution's rank structure for professional librarians. You should report here the maximum number of rank levels, reported in Part II for individual data, under the Rank column.

_____ 1 level (i.e., no differentiated levels)

_____ 2 levels

_____ 3 levels

_____ 4 levels

_____ 5 levels

_____ more than 5 levels (please specify the number of levels: _____)

3.   FOOTNOTES

3a.   Please list which libraries are included in the data submitted for the "general" libraries. These can be main campus libraries or branch campus libraries.

3b.   Please list which libraries are NOT included in the data submitted for the "general" libraries. These can be main campus libraries or branch campus libraries.

Please indicate any other explanatory information in footnotes. These additional footnotes, if necessary, should be placed in the space below or on attached pages.

Please submit the completed questionnaire to the web form at:
http://www.formspring.com/forms/?661042-c6BynijupA
by **September 30, 2009.**
For assistance, contact Martha Kyrillidou (martha@arl.org) or Les Bland (les@arl.org), or call 202-296-2296

ARL ANNUAL SALARY SURVEY 2009–2010
UNIVERSITY LIBRARY QUESTIONNAIRE

Note: This is a copy of the Excel form that you will submit electronically at:
http://www.formspring.com/forms/?661042-c6BynijupA

Part II: Individual Data

Reporting Library _____

Confidential
Detach before mailing to the ARL Office

Name/ID							Ethnicity	Race:	Race:	Race:	Race:	Race:	Race:
Line	Salary	Job	Sex	OEO cat	Yrs Exp	Rank	Percent	Hispanic or Latino	NatAm	Asian	Black	HawPI	White
1													
2													
3													
4													
5													
6													
7													
8													
9													
10													
11													
12													
13													
14													
15													
16													
17													
18													
19													
20													
21													
22													
23													
24													
25													

Duplicate this sheet if you need additional lines. Please return to the ARL Statistics and Measurement Program by **September 30, 2009**.
For assistance, contact Martha Kyrillidou (martha@arl.org) or Les Bland (les@arl.org), or call 202-296-2296.

NONUNIVERSITY LIBRARY QUESTIONNAIRE AND INSTRUCTIONS

ARL Annual Salary Survey 2009–2010

Nonuniversity Library Questionnaire

General Instructions for Completing the Questionnaire

1. This survey is concerned with the salaries of professional positions only. Since the criteria for determining professional status vary among libraries, there is no attempt to define the term "professional." Each library should report the salaries of those staff members it considers professionals, irrespective of membership in a collective bargaining unit, and including, when appropriate, staff who are not librarians in the strict sense of the term, such as systems analysts, budget officers, etc.

2. **Obtain the Word file.** These instructions assume that you have Microsoft Word available for use. If not, or if you have trouble opening the files in Word, please call the ARL Statistics and Measurement Program at (202) 296–2296 or e-mail les@arl.org.

3. The template Word file is available at: http://www.arl.org/stats/annualsurveys/salary/salform09.shtml. This is a generic, blank form that can hold your data. The file's name is "sal09_nuform.doc"; open the file and save it to your own computer by choosing "Save As" under the File menu. When saving the file, utilize ARL as the prefix, use 09 to designate the year (2009–2010), and change the "xxxx" in its name to your ARL institution code number, e.g., "ARL099975.doc."

4. Salaries should be reported for all filled positions. Vacant positions should be excluded from your report.

5. Report 2009–2010 salaries *as they exist on July 1, 2009*. If the library normally increases salaries at a date after July l, and the salary as of that later date is known or can be estimated (within $100 or so) by the time the questionnaire is due to be returned, please use the higher salary and footnote the effective date and/or whether the reported figures are known or estimated. Please do not hold up the reporting process for later salary adjustments.

6. The Median Salary is the salary that has an equal number of salaries above it and below it. In those libraries with an even number of positions, the median salary is the average of the two salaries that have an equal number of salaries above and below them.

7. The Beginning Professional Salary is the salary that would be paid to a professional without experience, not necessarily the lowest professional salary paid. In reporting the beginning salary, please use a figure that is actually used or likely to be used for entry–level librarians hired by your library.

8. Salaries should be reported for both full–time and part–time professional positions. However, salaries for part–time positions should be converted to their full–time equivalents before reporting; do not report the actual part–time salary paid.

9. Salaries should normally be reported on a 12–month basis. If an appointment is for 9 or 10 months at the option of the employee, the actual salary paid should be increased to its 12–month equivalent. However, if appointments of less than 12 months are required by the employer, report the actual salary paid.

10. The salaries for all professional positions should be included, regardless of whether the salaries come from regular library budget funds or from special funds such as research grants.

11. The salary figures should be straight gross salary figures. Do not include fringe benefits.

12. Explanatory footnotes to the reported figures may be provided when necessary. Footnotes will be included in the published survey.

13. Provide the name of the reporting library and the name of the person who prepares the report.

14. On the second page of the questionnaire (Part II) indicate the number of filled professional positions in each salary range for fiscal years 2008–2009 and 2009–2010.

15. **Use the newly available Web form for your data submission:**
(http://www.formspring.com/forms/?661053–c6BynijupA). Fill in Part I on the Web and upload your file for Part II through the same interface. <u>NOTE: You must complete the entire submission in a single session. The Web interface does **NOT** allow you to return and edit your information once it is submitted.</u>

Note: ARL is using the online services of FormSpring to collect the data. As part of its privacy policy, FormSpring pledges not to sell any collected information to third parties. For the complete FormSpring privacy policy, visit http://www.formspring.com/privacy.html. ARL also accepts Part I and Part II of the salary survey by e–mail attachment from those users who may be uncomfortable submitting the files in FormSpring.

Please Submit the Web form by September 30, 2009.

For assistance, contact Martha Kyrillidou (martha@arl.org) or Les Bland (les@arl.org) or
David Green (david@arl.org) or Gary Roebuck (gary@arl.org). Tel. 202–296–2296 or fax 202–872–0884.

ARL ANNUAL SALARY SURVEY 2009–2010

NONUNIVERSITY LIBRARY QUESTIONNAIRE

Note: This is a copy of the form that you will submit electronically at:
http://www.formspring.com/forms/?661053-c6BynijupA

Part I: Summary Data

Reporting Institution_____ Date Returned to ARL_____

Report Prepared by (name)_____

Title_____

Email address _____ Phone number_____

Contact person (if different) _____

Title_____

Email address _____ Phone number_____

1. Complete the table on the back of this sheet by indicating the number of filled or temporarily vacant professional positions in each salary range for fiscal years 2007–2008 and 2008–2009.

2. Median professional salary for fiscal year 2009–2010:   _____

3. Beginning professional salary for 2009–2010:   _____

4. Footnotes (please compare with footnotes from surveys of previous years)

    a. Law Library salaries are included.

        _____ Yes   _____ No   _____ We do not have a Law Library.

    b. Medical Library salaries are included.

        _____ Yes   _____ No   _____ We do not have a Medical Library.

    c. Branch libraries not included (please attach an additional sheet if necessary):

        _____
        _____

5. Other comments (please attach an additional sheet if necessary):

    _____

Part II Salaries:

Indicate the number of filled professional positions in each salary range for fiscal years 2007–2008 and 2008–2009. Submit this form electronically (after Part 1) at: http://www.formspring.com/forms/?661053-c6BynijupA

Salary Range	Number of Positions	
	2008–2009	2009–2010
More than 250,000		
200,000 – 250,000		
175,000 – 199,999		
150,000 – 174,999		
140,000 – 149,999		
130,000 – 139,999		
120,000 – 129,999		
110,000 – 119,999		
100,000 – 109,999		
95,000 – 99,999		
90,000 – 94,999		
85,000 – 89,999		
80,000 – 84,999		
76,000 – 79,999		
74,000 – 75,999		
72,000 – 73,999		
70,000 – 71,999		
68,000 – 69,999		
66,000 – 67,999		
64,000 – 65,999		
62,000 – 63,999		
60,000 – 61,999		
58,000 – 59,999		
56,000 – 57,999		
54,000 – 55,999		
52,000 – 53,999		
50,000 – 51,999		
48,000 – 49,999		
46,000 – 47,999		
44,000 – 45,999		
42,000 – 43,999		
40,000 – 41,999		
38,000 – 39,999		
36,000 – 37,999		
34,000 – 35,999		
32,000 – 33,999		
30,000 – 31,999		
less than 30,000		
Total Number of Positions		

Please submit the completed questionnaire to the Web form by **September 30, 2008.**
For assistance, contact Martha Kyrillidou (martha@arl.org) or Les Bland (les@arl.org) or
David Green (david@arl.org) or Gary Roebuck (gary@arl.org). Tel. 202–296–2296 or fax 202–872–0884.

Footnotes to the ARL Annual Salary Survey, 2009–2010

All data is as of 1 July 2009 unless otherwise noted.

ALABAMA

Libraries included: Amelia Gayle Gorgas Library, Angelo Bruno Business Library, McLure Education Library, Eric & Sarah Rodgers Library for Science & Engineering, and the W.S. Hoole Special Collections Library.

The listed Beginning Professional Salary (BPS) for the law library is with MLS & JD.

ALBERTA

The following libraries are included: Bibliographic Services, HT Coutts Education Library, Humanities & Social Sciences Library, Faculty Saint-Jean Library, Winspear Business Reference Library, Office of Staff Development and Training, Cameron Library (including Interlibrary Loans/Document Delivery, Financial Systems and Analysis, Science & Technology Library, Information Technology Resource Services).

ARIZONA

The following libraries are included: Main Campus Library, Science-Engineering Library, Fine Arts Library, Special Collections Library, and The Center for Creative Photography.

Data for the medical library includes the Health Sciences Library in Phoenix.

ARIZONA STATE

University Libraries include ASU Tempe campus, ASU West campus, ASU Polytechnic campus, ASU Phoenix Downtown campus, and the Law Library.

Beginning Professional Salary for the Law Library is $45,000 (entry level) and $50,000 with JD.

AUBURN

Includes the Main campus library, Architecture Library, and the Vet Med Library.

BOSTON

The main library and law library have an 8-step rank structure.

BOSTON COLLEGE

Includes the Tip O'Neill Jr. Library, Bapst Art Library, John J. Burns Library of Rare Books and Special Collections, School of Social Work Library, Educational Resource Center, School of Theology and Ministry Library, and the Law Library.

BRIGHAM YOUNG

The Harold B. Lee Library (main campus library) and the Howard W. Hunter Law Library are included in this survey.

BRITISH COLUMBIA

The following libraries are included: Art+Architecture+Planning, Asian Library, David Lam Library, Education Library, Irving K. Barber Learning Centre, Koerner Library, Law Library, Library Processing Centre (Technical Services, IST), Life Science Libraries: Biomedical Branch Library, Hamber Library, St. Paul's Hospital Library, Woodward Biomedical Library, Music Library, Okanagan Library, Rare Books & Special Collections, Robson Square, Science and Engineering, University Archives, and the Xwi7xwa Library (First Nations House of Learning).

Reading Rooms and Affiliated Libraries are not included.

The University of British Columbia Library system has no rank structure.

BROWN

Includes the John D. Rockefeller, Jr. Library, John Hay Library, Orwig Music Library, List Art Library, Sciences Library, and the John Carter Brown Library.

CALGARY
Main Library submission includes: Mackimmie Library; Gallagher Library of Geology & Geophysics; Business Library; Military Museum Library & Archives. Health Libraries include: Health Sciences Library and Health Information Network Knowledge Centres. The Law Library is also included.

CALIFORNIA, BERKELEY
The following libraries are included: Doe, Moffitt, Bancroft, Anthropology, Art History/Classics, Astronomy- Mathematics- Statistics, Bioscience and Natural Resources, Business & Economics, Chemistry, C.V. Starr East Asian Library (including Center for Chinese Studies), Earth Sciences, Education-Psychology, Engineering, Environmental Design, Music, Optometry, Physics, Public Health (including Health Sciences Information Services, and Occupational & Environmental Health), Social Welfare libraries, and the Northern Regional Library Facility.

The following libraries are not included: Architectural (Slide Library), Continuing Education of the Bar, Earthquake Engineering, Ethnic Studies, Giannini, Institute of Governmental Studies, Institute of Industrial Relations, Institute of International Studies, and the Institute of Transport Library.

Beginning 2004–2005, UCB salary figures include administrative stipends, where applicable.

CALIFORNIA, DAVIS
Includes Peter J. Shields Library (Davis Campus); Physical Sciences & Engineering Library (Davis Campus); Carlson Health Sciences Library (Davis Campus); Blaisdell Medical Center Library (Sacramento), and Agricultural & Resource Economics Library (Davis).

Librarians who are department heads have received administrative stipends since July 1, 1999, but these stipends were not included until this report. We are including those stipends in the department head's salaries (as reported) and we plan to continue to do so in the future.

CALIFORNIA, LOS ANGELES
Includes the Arts Library, College Library (Undergraduate Library), Eugene and Maxine Rosenfeld Management Library, Music Library, Richard C. Rudolph East Asian Library, Science & Engineering Library, Social Sciences and Humanities Library (Charles E. Young Research Library), and the Southern Regional Library Facility.

Includes data for 12 affiliated libraries on the UCLA campus including the 1) American Indian Studies Center, 2) Ralph M. Bunche African American Studies Center, 3) Asian American Studies Center, 4) Chicano Studies Research Center, 5) Ethnomusicology Archive, 6) Film & Television Archive, 7) Graduate School of Education & Information Studies, Department of Information Studies, 8) Institute for Social Science Research, 9) Latin American Center/Hispanic American Periodicals Index, 10) Olive View Medical Center, 11) Grace M. Hunt English Reading Room, and 12) William Andrews Clark Memorial Library.

Librarians who are department heads have received administrative stipends since January 1998; however, these stipends were not included in the salaries reported to ARL prior to 2003. Beginning with the 2003 survey, UCLA now includes those stipends in salaries reported for department heads. Interim department heads also receive stipends and these are reported in the survey.

The General Library Survey includes one Council of Library & Information Resources (CLIR) Fellows.

CALIFORNIA, RIVERSIDE
Includes the following: Rivera Library (serving the College of Humanities, Arts and Social Sciences, School of Education, and the School of Business Administration), Science Library (serving the College of Natural & Agricultural Sciences, the College of Engineering, and Biomedical Sciences), Palm Desert Campus Library (serving the Graduate School of Management & the College of Humanities, Arts, and Social Sciences).

Media and Music Libraries are not included (there are no librarian employees in these facilities).

CALIFORNIA, SAN DIEGO
Includes the following: Arts Libraries, Social Sciences & Humanities, International Relations & Pacific Studies, Scripps Institution of Oceanography, Science & Engineering, Special Collections Library, Biomedical Library, and the Medical Center Library.

CALIFORNIA, SANTA BARBARA
Includes the Main and Arts Libraries.

The UCSB library has 8 levels in its rank structure.

CASE WESTERN RESERVE
Kelvin Smith Library, Kulas Music Library, Mandel School of Applied Social Sciences Library, and the Harris Library are included.

CHICAGO
All libraries, including law and medicine, are incorporated in this report.

CINCINNATI
Includes all main campus libraries.

Branch campus libraries are not included.

CANADA INSTITUTE OF SCIENTIFIC AND TECHNICAL INFORMATION
All branch libraries are included.

All values were reported in Canadian Dollars.

COLORADO
The following libraries are included: Norlin Library, Music Library, Earth Sciences Library, Business Library, Math/Physics Library, Engineering Library, and the Law Library.

CONNECTICUT
The Main, Law, Pharmacy, and Music & Dramatic Arts libraries are included in this report.

The Beginning Professional Salary (BPS) for the Law Library has decreased because of the severe economic downturn.

CORNELL
Africana, Engineering, Entomology, Fine Arts, Geneva Experiment Station, Hotel Administration, Management, Mann Library, Math, Music, ILR, Olin/Kroch/Uris, Physical Sciences, Veterinary Medicine, Law, and Health Science libraries are included in this survey.

DARTMOUTH
Libraries included in this report: Baker-Berry Library, Feldberg Business & Engineering Library, Kresge Physical Sciences Library, Paddock Music Library, Rauner Special Collections Library, Sherman Art Library Storage Library, Dana Biomedical Library, and the Matthews-Fuller Health Sciences Library.

DELAWARE
Excludes the salary data of University of Delaware libraries not reporting directly to the Director of Libraries.

DUKE
The following libraries are included: Perkins/Bostock; Lilly, Music; Library Services Center; Divinity; Rare Book, Manuscript and Special Collections, University Archives, Law, and Health libraries.

The University did not authorize a merit pool for Fiscal Year 2010 (1 July 2009 – 30 June 2010). In lieu of annual merit increases in 2010, employees who have achieved a successful or exceptional rating on the 2008–2009 performance evaluation and who earn $50,000 per year or less will receive a one-time $1,000 payment (calculations based on a 1.0 FTE). There will be no merit increase or one time payment for University employees making more than $50,000 per year. Librarians earning less than the $45K minimum will be adjusted appropriately.

EMORY
The General Libraries, Theology Library, and Oxford College Library (Emory's two-year college) are included in this survey.

FLORIDA
Main libraries included Humanities and Social Sciences Library; Science Library; Journalism Library; Music Library; Architecture and Fine Arts Library; Education Library; Education Library; Latin America Collection; and the Maps Library.

Medical libraries data includes the main Health Science Center Library; a satellite branch in another city; and the Veterinary Medicine Reading Room.

The Main and Medical libraries data is reported separately for this survey, but the systems were integrated in 2009, and now all libraries, with the exception of Law, report through the Dean of University Libraries.

For the purpose of this survey, Main and Medical libraries both have 7 rank levels.

FLORIDA STATE
The Allen Music Library, Goldstein College of Information Library are included with the main, law, and medical libraries in this report.

Panama City, Florida Branch, and the Sarasota Ringling branch libraries are not included.

We have a six-level rank system: 0- Dean; 1- Assistant Instructor; 2- Associate Instructor; 3- Instruction librarian; 4- Assistant Librarian; 5- Associate Librarian; 6- University Librarian.

GEORGETOWN
Lauinger Library (Main), Woodstock Theological Library, Blommer Science Library, and the Bio-ethics Library are all included in this submission.

GEORGIA
Libraries included: Main Library, Science Library, Map Library, Student Learning Center Library, Curriculum Learning Center Library, several reading rooms, and experimental station libraries located throughout the State of Georgia.

The University of Georgia Law Library uses 9 levels in its rank structure.

GUELPH
The following main libraries are included: McLaughlin Library, and the OVC Learning Commons/Library. Branch Campus libraries included: Guelph Humber Learning Commons/Library and the Ridgetown Campus Library.

All salary values were reported in Canadian Dollars ($CAD).

Individual rank data have been included only for professional librarians. Rank structure as follows: Library Director assigned rank = 0; Assistant Librarian assigned rank = 1; Associate Librarian assigned rank = 2; Librarian assigned rank = 3; Non-librarian professionals assigned rank = 9.

HARVARD
Includes the Law and Medical libraries as well as the Villa i Tatti and the Hellenic Center Libraries.

Excludes the Bilioteca Berenson (Florence, Italy) and the Dunbarton Oaks Research Libraries (Washington, DC).

Harvard uses a 9-step rank structure.

The salaries for Head of the Medical and Law libraries do not include compensation for the research and professorial duties of this position, yet they are considered full time.

HAWAII
Includes the Hamilton, Sinclair Libraries, and the Law library.

Both the Law Library and the Health Sciences Library are independent from the main university library and the directors report to their respective deans (Law and Medicine).

HOUSTON
The following are included: M.D. Anderson Library, Architecture and Art Library, Music Library, Weston A. Pettey Optometry Library, and the Pharmacy Library.

HOWARD
Founders Library and associated branches, including both the Law and the Louis Stokes Library (Health Sciences).

The Moorland-Spingarn Research center is not included.

The Louis Stokes Health Sciences Library (LSHSL) is independent from the "general libraries" and is not a branch. However, we report these statistics with the general library.

ILLINOIS, CHICAGO

The medical libraries at Chicago, Peoria, Rockford, and Urbana are not included.

Illinois, Chicago has 6 levels for professional librarians: 6= Professor, 5= Associate Professor, 4= Assistant Professor, including visiting appointments, 3= Clinical Assistant Professor, 2= Instructor (Resident, Professional Library Associate), 1= Instructor (currently all 1 ranks are vacant).

INDIANA

Main campus libraries and the Indianapolis School of Law Library are included.

Not included: Dentistry and Medicine Library; IUPUI University Library; Herron School of Art Library, Columbus Library, and Science & Engineering Library; and other campuses libraries at IU-East, IU-Kokomo, IU-Northwest, IU-Southeast, IU-South Bend, and IPFW-Fort Wayne.

IOWA

The following libraries are included: Main, Art, Biological Sciences, Engineering, Geoscience, Math, Music, Physics, and Psychology, Health Sciences, and Law.

All libraries mentioned above are on the same campus.

IOWA STATE

Includes Parks (main library) and the Veterinary Library.

JOHNS HOPKINS

Includes the Sheridan Libraries, Welch Medical Library, Friedheim Library, and the School of Advanced International Studies Library (SAIS).

KANSAS

Includes Regents Center Library, Edwards Campus (Overland Park, KS).

Excludes University of Kansas School of Medicine, Farha Library (Wichita, KS).

KENT STATE

Includes all libraries on the Kent State Kent campus: Main, Architecture, Chemistry/Physics, Fashion, Map, Music.

Includes libraries at Kent State branch campuses: Ashtabula, East Liverpool, Geauga, Salem, Stark, Trumbull, Tuscarawas.

The starting BPS we reported is for tenure-track faculty only. This figure is a significant increase over 2008–2009 and was determined by the university's collective bargaining agreement.

KENTUCKY

Includes the following: William T. Young Library (Main Campus Library), Agricultural Information Center, Design Library, Education Library, Engineering Library, Equine Library, Fine Arts Library, Science Library, and the Kentucky Transportation Center Library.

LIBRARY OF CONGRESS

Salaries include both professional and administrative positions.

LOUISVILLE

Main, Music, Art, University Archives, Law, and Kornhauser Health Sciences Library are included.

MCMASTER
Includes the Innis Library, H.G. Thode Library and the Mills Memorial Library.

MANITOBA
Includes: William R. Newman Agriculture Library, Architecture/Fine Arts Library, Archives & Special Collections, Elizabeth Dafoe Library, Father Harold Drake Library, St. John's College Library, Donald W. Craik Engineering Library, E.K. Williams Law Library, Albert D. Cohen Management Library, Eckhardt-Gramatte Music Library, Sciences and Technology Library, Neil John Maclean Health Sciences Library, Bill Larson Library, Carolyn Sifton-Helene Fuld Library, Concordia Hospital Library, J.W. Crane Memorial Library, Misercordia Health Centre Library, Riverview Health Centre Virtual Library, Seven Oaks General Hospital Library, and the Victoria General Hospital Library.

MASSACHUSETTS
The DuBois, Integrated Sciences & Engineering, and Image Collection Libraries are included.

MIAMI
Rank structure for the main library is a 6-step structure (1–6).

The data submitted for Health Sciences are for the Calder and Psychiatry libraries.

MICHIGAN
Includes Hatcher Graduate; Shapiro Undergraduate; Shapiro Science; Art, Architecture & Engineering; Askwith Media; Area Programs; Asia; Map; Special Collections; Spatial & Numeric Data Services; Fine Arts; Social Work; Muesums; Music; Government Documents; Papyrology; Health Sciences Libraries; Law; Kresge Business Administration; Clements; Bentley and Gerald Ford Presidential Library.

Law Library beginning professional salary: $48,000 for MILS degree only; $60,000 for JD and MILS.

MICHIGAN STATE
Includes the Main, Biomedical, Physical Sciences, Math, Veterinary Medicine, Business, and Engineering libraries.

MISSOURI
Includes Main, Journalism, Engineering, Veterinary Medicine, and Archives Libraries.

MIT
MIT Libraries include: Barker Engineering Library, Science Library, Rotch Library for Architecture and Planning, Dewey Library for Management and Social Science, Humanities Library, Lewis Music Library (branch of Humanities), Rotch Visual Collections (branch of Rotch), and Institute Archives and Special Collections.

The number of levels in our rank structure is 9. Rank level 1 is currently vacant.

MONTREAL
Libraries included: Environmental Development, Library and Information Sciences, Botany, Chemistry, Educational Resources, Education-Communication-Psychology-Psychoeducation-Biology, Geography, Kinesiology, Humanities and Social Sciences, Rare Books and Special Collections, Mathematics and Computer Sciences, Veterinary, Music, Optometry, Physics, École polytechnique Library, Law, Health, and Paramedics.

NATIONAL LIBRARY OF MEDICINE
Data reported by the Federal fiscal year, which runs October 1 to September 30 of each calendar year.

NEW MEXICO
University of New Mexico Libraries include: Centennial Science & Engineering Library, Fine Arts & Design Library, Parish Memorial Library, Zimmerman Library, Law Library, and the Health Sciences Library.

Not included: Gallup Campus Branch Library, Los Alamos Campus Branch Library, Taos Campus Branch Library, Valencia Campus Branch Library.

Definition of professional positions have been recalibrated to better represent professional activities and education. Public Service Librarian positions includes staff who function as "Ambassadors" and Teachers at a level above specialist.

NEW YORK

Includes: Elmer Holmes Bobst Library, Institute of Fine Arts, Courant Institute of Mathematical Sciences Library, Institute for Studies of the Ancient World, Real Estate Library, Law School Library, and the Medical School Library.

NYU's three ranks are indicated as follows: 1 - Library Associate; 2 - Assistant Curator; 3 - Associate Curator.

NORTH CAROLINA STATE

Includes: D.H. Hill (main) Library, Design Library, Natural Resources Library, Textiles Library, and the Veterinary Medicine Library.

NORTHWESTERN

Includes the Main Library, Science & Engineering Library, Law Librar,y and Medical Library.

NOTRE DAME

Hesburgh Library (Main) includes: Architecture Library, Art Image Library, Business Information Center, Chemistry/Physics Library, Engineering Library, Kellogg/Kroc Information Center, and Mathematics Library. In addition, the Kresge Law Library has also been reported.

OHIO

Includes the main campus (Main Library plus Music/Dance Library) and five regional campus libraries (Eastern, Southern, Chillicothe, Lancaster, and Zanesville).

OHIO STATE

Includes all main campus libraries, regional campus libraries, and libraries of the Agricultural Technical Institute and the Ohio Agricultural Research and development center.

Several specialized department research libraries on the main campus which are not part of the University Libraries system are not included.

OKLAHOMA STATE

Includes the following main campus libraries: Edmon Low Library, Mary L. Williams Curriculum Materials Library, Cunningham Architecture Library, Brock Memorial Library at the Center for Veterinary Health Sciences, and the OSU Center for Health Sciences Library.

Includes the following branch campuses: OSU-Okmulgee Library, OSU-Oklahoma City Library, OSU-Tulsa Library.

An error was made during the processing of Oklahoma State's medical library for the 2008–2009 Salary Survey. An incorrect survey size of 8 "professionals" was reported—4 was the proper figure.

OREGON

Includes: Knight Library (main), Science Library, Architecture & Allied Arts Library, Portland Library & Learning Commons, and the Law Library.

Explanation of our rank system: 1 = Assistant Professor, 2 = Associate Professor, 3 = Professor, 9 = Unranked, 0 = Dean of Libraries.

PENNSYLVANIA

Includes: Museum, Fine Arts, Physical Sciences, Center for Advanced Judaic Studies, Rare Book & Manuscript, Music, Business, and Law Libraries.

PENNSYLVANIA STATE

All the libraries at the University Park (Main Campus) are included. Libraries at the following branches: Abington, Altoona, Beaver, Berks, Brandywine, DuBois, Erie, Fayette, Great Valley, Greater Allegheny, Harrisburg, Hazleton, Lehigh Valley, Mont Alto, New Kensington, Shenango, Schuylkill, Wilkes-Barre, Worthington-Scranton, and York are also included.

PITTSBURGH

Includes the University Library System and excludes branch campuses at Titusville, Johnstown, Bradford, and Greensburg.

PRINCETON

Includes the Firestone Library, Marquand Library of Art & Archaeology, Mendel Music Library, Architecture Library, Stokes Library, East Asian Library, Engineering Library, Princeton Plasma Physics Library, Lewis Library, Psychology Library, and the Cotsen Children's Library.

The Lewis Library has incorporated the following branch libraries: Science and Technology, Biology and Life Sciences, Chemistry, Astrophysics, Physics, Math, and Geographical Sciences.

The Beginning Professional Salary (BPS) has increased from that paid in 2008–2009.

PURDUE

Includes the library system on the West Lafayette campus, consisting of 11 subject libraries, an undergraduate library, and an archives and special collections unit.

Excludes libraries at the regional campuses: Purdue North Central (Westville), Purdue Calumet (Hammond), and Indiana University-Purdue University, Fort Wayne.

RICE

In this reporting period, Rice University provided raises only to those making less than $60,000 yearly.

ROCHESTER

Includes River Campus Libraries, Edward G. Miner Medical Library, and the Sibley Music Library.

RUTGERS

Includes the Newark Law Campus, Camden Law Campus, Research and Instructional Services, John Cotton Dana Library, Paul Robeson Library, Technical and Automated Services, Alexander Library, Mabel Smith Douglas Library, Kilmer Library, and the Library of Science and Medicine (and branches).

Excludes the School for Management and Labor Relations, and the Center for Alcohol Studies.

Salaries are unchanged from last year (2008–2009) because negotiated raises have been delayed (Newark Law Library).

SASKATCHEWAN

Includes Main Library, Education Library, and the Natural Sciences, Law, Medical, VetMed, and Engineering libraries.

Numbers of employees based upon those working at the library as of 1 July 2009.

SOUTH CAROLINA

Includes the Thomas Cooper Library, South Caroliniana Library, Moving Image Research Collection, South Carolina Political Collections, Music Library, Math Library, Business Library, Law Library, and Medical Library.

SOUTHERN CALIFORNIA

Includes all main campus libraries as well as the Norris Medical Library.

Beginning professional salary remains the same as 2008–2009.

SUNY-ALBANY

Libraries included are University Library, Science Library, and Dewey Graduate Library.

Salaries include 3% union-negotiated increase, administrative stipends and SL-2 ranks. Vacant positions are not included. We have included our SL-2 ranks in this report so our survey size has increased from 2008–2009.

SUNY-BUFFALO
Includes the Arts and Sciences Libraries, Music Library, Special Collections (Archives, Poetry, and Rare Books).

Excludes temporary hires, employees at the SL-2 salary level, and classified staff.

SYRACUSE
Includes the Main campus library, Science and Technology library, Geology Library, Law Library, and the Math Library.

TEMPLE
Includes: Paley Library; Science, Engineering & Architecture Library; Charles L. Blockson Afro-American Collection; Ambler Campus Library.

Main Library minimum beginning professional salary of $44,044 is based on an 11-month contract. The minimum for a 10-month contract is $40,150.

TENNESSEE
Main (University of Tennessee) Library, Memphis Health Sciences Library, and Knoxville Hospital Preston Medical Library are included.

The Memphis Health Sciences Library has a 4-rank salary structure and the Knoxville Hospital has a 3-rank structure.

Beginning salary for Memphis Hospital is $45,000 and $38,000 for Knoxville Hospital.

TEXAS
Figures are as of August 31, 2009. Included are the Dolph Briscoe Center for American History, Tarlton Law Library, the Harry Ransom Humanities Research Center, and the University of Texas Libraries.

TEXAS A&M
The following libraries are included: Sterling C. Evans Library, Library Annex, Cushing Memorial Library, Technical Reference Center (Architecture Library), Medical Sciences Library, West Campus Library, Policy Sciences and Economics Library, Jack K. Williams Library (Galveston), and the Texas A&M University Library at Qatar.

The 1's (Lecturers) and 2's (Senior Lecturers) in our rank structure are non-tenured track appointments with a different salary schedule than our tenure track employees (3 - Assistant Professor, 4 - Associate Professor, 5 - Professor). 9's are Library professionals that work in specialized areas and have a different salary structure than either the tenured or non-tenured appointments.

TEXAS TECH
The Law Library reports 4 levels in their rank structure and the Health Sciences Library reports 5 levels in their rank structure.

Figures reported are as of 09/01/2009.

TORONTO
The proposed July 01, 2009 across-the-board pay increase has not yet been finalized.

Salary increases reflect movement within the rank structure (e.g., promotions).

UTAH
Includes the Main Library, Eccles Health Sciences Library, and the Quinney Law Library.

The Spencer S. Eccles Library is the main medical library. It is not a branch library reporting to Marriott Library. The medical library reports directly to the VP of Health at the University of Utah.

VANDERBILT
The data submitted includes the Central Library, Divinity Library, Peabody Library, Management Library, Science & Engineering Library, Special Collections and University Archives, centralized Technical Services, Library Information Technology Services, Law Library, Health Sciences Library, Library Administration, and the Television News Archive.

VIRGINIA

Includes the following University of Virginia Libraries: Alderman (Main), Astronomy, Biology/Psychology, Chemistry, Clemons (Undergraduate), Education, Fiske Kimball Fine Arts, Math, Music, Physics, Brown Science/Engineering, Small Special Collections, Darden Graduate Business, Claude Moore Health Sciences, and the Authur Morris Law Library.

Excludes the John Cook Wyllie Library at the University of Virginia College at Wise.

WASHINGTON

Includes librarians on the Seattle, Bothell, and Tacoma campuses of the University of Washington.

WASHINGTON STATE

Includes all main campus libraries and the following branches: WSU-Riverpoint Campus, WSU-Tri-Cities, WSU-Vancouver, and the WSU-Energy Library.

WASHINGTON UNIVERSITY-ST. LOUIS

Includes the Central Library and departmental libraries in Art & Architecture, Biology, Business, Chemistry, Earth & Planetary Sciences, East Asian, Music, Physics, Social Work, and West Campus Library. The Law and Medical libraries are also included.

WATERLOO

Includes the Dana Porter; Davis Centre; University Map Library, and Musagetes Architecture Libraries.

We have a 6-level rank structure.

WAYNE STATE

The "general libraries" include the Purdy/Kresge Library, Science and Engineering Library, and the Undergraduate Library.

The libraries not included in the "general libraries" are the Neef Law Library and the Shiffman Medical Library, which are reported separately, and the Reuther Archives of Labor and Urban Affairs, which is not included in this report.

The decrease in the number of professionals reported (decreased from 2008–2009) is not the result of lost positions. It stems from our having looked more closely at which staff members were classified as professionals. The examination revealed that a certain level of staff that we have consistently counted as support staff when responding to the ARL Annual Survey were being counted as professional staff when responding to the Salary Survey. In order to be consistent and to accurately portray our libraries, we have now corrected this.

WESTERN ONTARIO

The D.B. Weldon Library, Business Library, Education Library, Music Library, Allyn & Betty Taylor Library are included in this survey.

Affiliated College Libraries are not included. These are King's University College Library, Huron University College Library, and the Brescia University College Library.

July 1, 2009 salary increases are currently under negotiation.

WISCONSIN

Includes General Library System (Memorial, Steenbock, College, Art, Music, Special Collections, Geology, Geography, Biology, Physics, Social Work, Business, Chemistry, Math, Social Science Reading Room), Law, Medical, and the Wendt Engineering Library.

Our rank structure is as follows: 1 = Associate Academic Librarian, 2 = Academic Librarian, 3 = Senior Academic Librarian, 4 = Distinguished Academic Librarian, 5 = Assistant/Associate Director, 6 = Director of the Steenbock, College, Memorial, Wendt, Law or Medical Libraries, 7 = Deputy Director General Library System, 0 = Director General Library.

YALE

Includes: the African Collection, Anthropology Library, Area Studies Library, Arts Library, Arts of the Book Collection, Astronomy Library, Babylonian Collection, Bass Library, Beinecke Rare Book and Manuscript Library, Center for British Art, Chemistry Library, Classics Library, Divinity School Library, Drama Library, East Asia Library, Economic Growth Center Collection, Engineering and Applied Science Library, Epidemiology and Public Health Library, Film Study Center, Forestry and Environmental Studies Library, Fortunoff Video Archive for Holocaust Testimonies, Geographic Information Systems (GIS) at Yale, Geology Library, Government Documents and Information Center, Historical Sound Recordings, Judaica Collection, Kline Science Library, Latin American Collection, Lewis Walpole Library, Library Shelving Facility, Manuscripts and Archives at SML, Map Collection, Mathematics Library, Medical Historical Library, Microform Reading Room, Mudd Library, Music Library, Near Eastern Collection, Newspaper Reading Room, Nursing Library and Information Resources, Ornithology Library, Slavic and East European Collection, Social Science Libraries and Information Services, Southeast Asia Collection, Special Collections at Yale, Sterling Memorial Library, Visual Resources Collection, Yale Center for British Art, Medical Library, and the Law Library.

YORK

Please note that a new faculty collective agreement has been negotiated and beginning salary for 2009–2010 remains at the same level as 2008–2009 until details are finalized.

ARL Member Libraries as of January 1, 2010

The Association of Research Libraries (ARL) represents the interests of 124 libraries that serve major North American research institutions. ARL operates as a forum for the exchange of ideas and as an agent for collective action to influence the forces affecting the ability of these libraries to meet the future needs of scholarship. The ARL Statistics and Measurement program is organized around identifying, collecting, analyzing, and distributing quantifiable information describing the characteristics of research libraries. The program offers publications and special member services, and collaborates with other national and international library statistics programs.

Institution	Category	Full Name of Institution	Location
Alabama	S	University of Alabama	Tuscaloosa, Alabama
Alberta	C	University of Alberta	Edmonton, Alberta
Arizona	S	University of Arizona	Tucson, Arizona
Arizona State	S	Arizona State University	Tempe, Arizona
Auburn	S	Auburn University	Auburn, Alabama
Boston	P	Boston University	Boston, Massachusetts
Boston College	P	Boston College	Boston, Massachusetts
Brigham Young	P	Brigham Young University	Provo, Utah
British Columbia	C	University of British Columbia	Vancouver, British Columbia
Brown	P	Brown University	Providence, Rhode Island
Berkeley, California	S	University of California, Berkeley	California, Berkeley
Calgary	C	University of Calgary	Calgary, Alberta
California, Davis	S	University of California, Davis	Davis, California
California, Irvine	S	University of California, Irvine	Irvine, California
California, Los Angeles	S	University of California, Los Angeles	Los Angeles, California
California, Riverside	S	University of California, Riverside	Riverside, California
California, San Diego	S	University of California, San Diego	La Jolla, California
California, Santa Barbara	S	University of California, Santa Barbara	Santa Barbara, California
Case Western Reserve	P	Case Western Reserve University	Cleveland, Ohio
Chicago	P	University of Chicago	Chicago, Illinois
Cincinnati	S	University of Cincinnati	Cincinnati, Ohio
Colorado	S	University of Colorado	Boulder, Colorado
Colorado State	S	Colorado State University	Fort Collins, Colorado
Columbia	P	Columbia University	New York, New York
Connecticut	S	University of Connecticut	Storrs, Connecticut
Cornell	P	Cornell University	Ithaca, New York
Dartmouth	P	Dartmouth College	Hanover, New Hampshire
Delaware	S	University of Delaware	Newark, Delaware
Duke	P	Duke University	Durham, North Carolina
Emory	P	Emory University	Atlanta, Georgia
Florida	S	University of Florida	Gainesville, Florida
Florida State	S	Florida State University	Tallahassee, Florida
George Washington	P	George Washington University	Washington, DC
Georgetown	P	Georgetown University	Washington, DC

Institution	Category	Full Name of Institution	Location
Georgia	S	University of Georgia	Athens, Georgia
Georgia Tech	S	Georgia Institute of Technology	Atlanta, Georgia
Guelph	C	University of Guelph	Guelph, Ontario
Harvard	P	Harvard University	Cambridge, Massachusetts
Hawaii	S	University of Hawaii	Honolulu, Hawaii
Houston	S	University of Houston	Houston, Texas
Howard	P	Howard University	Washington, DC
Illinois, Chicago	S	University of Illinois at Chicago	Chicago, Illinois
Illinois, Urbana	S	University of Illinois at Urbana	Urbana, Illinois
Indiana	S	Indiana University	Bloomington, Indiana
Iowa	S	University of Iowa	Iowa City, Iowa
Iowa State	S	Iowa State University	Ames, Iowa
Johns Hopkins	P	Johns Hopkins University	Baltimore, Maryland
Kansas	S	University of Kansas	Lawrence, Kansas
Kent State	S	Kent State University	Kent, Ohio
Kentucky	S	University of Kentucky	Lexington, Kentucky
Laval	C	Laval University	Quebec, Quebec
Louisiana State	S	Louisiana State University	Baton Rouge, Louisiana
Louisville	S	University of Louisville	Louisville, Kentucky
McGill	C	McGill University	Montreal, Quebec
McMaster	C	McMaster University	Hamilton, Ontario
Manitoba	C	University of Manitoba	Winnipeg, Manitoba
Maryland	S	University of Maryland	College Park, Maryland
Massachusetts	S	University of Massachusetts	Amherst, Massachusetts
MIT	P	Massachusetts Institute of Technology	Cambridge, Massachusetts
Miami	P	University of Miami	Coral Gables, Florida
Michigan	S	University of Michigan	Ann Arbor, Michigan
Michigan State	S	Michigan State University	East Lansing, Michigan
Minnesota	S	University of Minnesota	Minneapolis, Minnesota
Missouri	S	University of Missouri	Columbia, Missouri
Montreal	C	University of Montreal	Montreal, Quebec
Nebraska	S	University of Nebraska-Lincoln	Lincoln, Nebraska
New Mexico	S	University of New Mexico	Albuquerque, New Mexico
New York	P	New York University	New York, New York
North Carolina	S	University of North Carolina	Chapel Hill, North Carolina
North Carolina State	S	North Carolina State University	Raleigh, North Carolina
Northwestern	P	Northwestern University	Evanston, Illinois
Notre Dame	P	University of Notre Dame	Notre Dame, Indiana
Ohio	S	Ohio University	Athens, Ohio
Ohio State	S	Ohio State University	Columbus, Ohio
Oklahoma	S	University of Oklahoma	Norman, Oklahoma
Oklahoma State	S	Oklahoma State University	Stillwater, Oklahoma

Institution	Category	Full Name of Institution	Location
Oregon	S	University of Oregon	Eugene, Oregon
Pennsylvania	P	University of Pennsylvania	Philadelphia, Pennsylvania
Pennsylvania State	S	Pennsylvania State University	University Park, Pennsylvania
Pittsburgh	S	University of Pittsburgh	Pittsburgh, Pennsylvania
Princeton	P	Princeton University	Princeton, New Jersey
Purdue	S	Purdue University	West Lafayette, Indiana
Queen's	C	Queen's University	Kingston, Ontario
Rice	P	Rice University	Houston, Texas
Rochester	P	University of Rochester	Rochester, New York
Rutgers	S	Rutgers University	New Brunswick, New Jersey
Saskatchewan	C	University of Saskatchewan	Saskatoon, Saskatchewan
South Carolina	S	University of South Carolina	Columbia, South Carolina
Southern California	P	University of Southern California	Los Angeles, California
Southern Illinois	S	Southern Illinois University	Carbondale, Illinois
SUNY-Albany	S	University at Albany, State University of New York	Albany, New York
SUNY-Buffalo	S	University at Buffalo, State University of New York	Buffalo, New York
SUNY-Stony Brook	S	State University of New York at Stony Brook	Stony Brook, New York
Syracuse	P	Syracuse University	Syracuse, New York
Temple	S	Temple University	Philadelphia, Pennsylvania
Tennessee	S	University of Tennessee	Knoxville, Tennessee
Texas	S	University of Texas	Austin, Texas
Texas A&M	S	Texas A&M University	College Station, Texas
Texas Tech	S	Texas Tech University	Lubbock, Texas
Toronto	C	University of Toronto	Toronto, Ontario
Tulane	P	Tulane University	New Orleans, Louisiana
Utah	S	University of Utah	Salt Lake City, Utah
Vanderbilt	P	Vanderbilt University	Nashville, Tennessee
Virginia	S	University of Virginia	Charlottesville, Virginia
Virginia Tech	S	Virginia Polytechnic Institute & State University	Blacksburg, Virginia
Washington	S	University of Washington	Seattle, Washington
Washington State	S	Washington State University	Pullman, Washington
Washington U.-St. Louis	P	Washington University	St. Louis, Missouri
Waterloo	C	University of Waterloo	Waterloo, Ontario
Wayne State	S	Wayne State University	Detroit, Michigan
Western Ontario	C	University of Western Ontario	London, Ontario
Wisconsin	S	University of Wisconsin	Madison, Wisconsin
Yale	P	Yale University	New Haven, Connecticut
York	C	York University	North York, Ontario
Boston Public Library	N	Boston Public Library	Boston, Massachusetts
Canada Inst. SciTech Info.	X	Canada Inst. for Scientific & Technical Information	Ottawa, Ontario
Center for Research Libs.	N	Center for Research Libraries	Chicago, Illinois

Institution	Category	Full Name of Institution	Location
Library of Congress	N	Library of Congress	Washington, DC
Natl. Agricultural Lib.	N	National Agricultural Library	Beltsville, Maryland
Lib. & Archives Canada	X	Library and Archives Canada	Ottawa, Ontario
Natl. Library of Medicine	N	National Library of Medicine	Bethesda, Maryland
New York Public Library	N	New York Public Library	New York, New York
New York State Library	N	New York State Library	Albany, New York
Smithsonian Institution	N	Smithsonian Institution	Washington, DC

S – U.S. public university
P – U.S. private university
C – Canadian university
N – U.S. nonuniversity
X – Canadian nonuniversity

TABLE NUMBERING CHANGES 1998–1999 TO 1999–2000

From 1998–1999 to 1999–2000 a number of new tables were added to *ARL Annual Salary Survey* publication and some old tables were renumbered. As a result of these changes, a new section was added, entitled **US ARL University Libraries,** which includes Tables 26 and 29. Two new tables showing averages for all US and Canadian institutions were also included as Table 3 and Table 4. The table below maps the old table-numbering scheme to the new one for purposes of comparison.

Old	New	
		SALARY LEVELS FOR STAFF IN ARL LIBRARIES
1	1	Distribution by Salary Level
12	2	Salary Trends in ARL University Libraries
N/A	3	Salary Trends in US ARL University Libraries
N/A	4	Salary Trends in Canadian ARL University Libraries
		ARL NONUNIVERSITY LIBRARIES
2	5	Median and Beginning Professional Salaries in ARL Nonuniversity Libraries
3	6	Salary Trends in ARL Nonuniversity Libraries
		ARL UNIVERSITY LIBRARIES
4	7	Filled Positions; Average, Median, Beginning Professional Salaries, And Average Years of Professional Experience in ARL University Libraries, FY 1999–2000
5	8	Beginning Professional Salaries in ARL University Libraries; Rank Order Table, FY 1998–1999
6	9	Beginning Professional Salaries in ARL University Libraries; Rank Order Table, FY 1999–2000
7	10	Median Professional Salaries in ARL University Libraries; Rank Order Table, FY 1998–1999
8	11	Median Professional Salaries in ARL University Libraries; Rank Order Table, FY 1999–2000
9	12	Average Professional Salaries in ARL University Libraries; Rank Order Table, FY 1998–1999
10	13	Average Professional Salaries in ARL University Libraries; Rank Order Table, FY 1999–2000
11	14	Average, Median, and Beginning Professional Salaries in ARL University Libraries; Summary of Rankings, FYs 1996–1997 to 1999–2000
13	15	Distribution of Professional Staff in ARL University Libraries by Salary and Position, FY 1999–2000
14	16	Distribution of Professional Staff in ARL University Libraries by Salary, Sex, and Position, FY 1999–2000
15	17	Number and Average Salaries of ARL University Librarians by Position and Sex, FY 1999–2000
17	18	Number and Average Years of Experience of ARL University Librarians by Position and Sex, FY 1999–2000

Old	New	
19	19	Number and Average Salaries of ARL University Librarians by Years of Experience and Sex, FY 1999–2000
21	20	Average Salaries of ARL University Librarians by Years of Experience, FY 1999–2000
22	21	Number and Average Salaries of ARL University Librarians by Position and Type of Institution, FY 1999–2000
22b	22	Years of Experience of ARL University Librarians by Position and Type of Institution, FY 1999–2000
23	23	Number and Average Salaries of ARL University Librarians by Position and Size of Professional Staff, FY 1999–2000
23b	24	Years of Experience of ARL University Librarians by Position and Size of Professional Staff, FY 1999–2000
24	25	Average Salaries of ARL University Librarians by Position and Geographic Region, FY 1999–2000

US ARL University Libraries

Old	New	
N/A	26	Average Salaries of US ARL University Librarians by Position and Years of Experience, FY 1999–2000

US ARL University Libraries

Old	New	
16	27	Number and Average Salaries of Minority US ARL University Librarians by Position and Sex, FY 1999–2000
18	28	Number and Average Years of Experience of Minority US ARL University Librarians by Position and Sex, FY 1999–2000
N/A	29	Number and Average Salaries of US ARL University Librarians by Years of Experience and Sex, FY 1999–2000
20	30	Number and Average Salaries of Minority US ARL University Librarians by Years of Experience and Sex, FY 1999–2000

Canadian ARL University Libraries

Old	New	
25	31	Filled Positions; Average, Median, and Beginning Professional Salaries; and Average Years of Professional Experience in Canadian ARL University Libraries, FY 1999–2000
26	32	Number and Average Salaries of Canadian ARL University Librarians by Position and Sex, FY 1999–2000
27	33	Number and Average Years of Experience of Canadian ARL University Librarians by Position and Sex, FY 1999–2000
28	34	Number and Average Salaries of Canadian ARL University Librarians by Years of Experience and Sex, FY 1999–2000

ARL University Medical Libraries

Old	New	
29	35	Filled Positions; Average, Median, Beginning Professional Salaries; and Average Years of Professional Experience in ARL University Medical Libraries, FY 1999–2000
30	36	Beginning Professional Salaries in ARL University Medical Libraries; Rank Order Table, FY 1999–2000

7580768R0

Made in the USA
Charleston, SC
20 March 2011